THE
LIMITS
OF JUSTICE

A Sociological Analysis

Lydia Voigt
William E. Thornton

UNIVERSITY
PRESS OF
AMERICA

LANHAM • NEW YORK • LONDON

Copyright © 1984 by

University Press of America,™ Inc.

4720 Boston Way
Lanham, MD 20706

3 Henrietta Street
London WC2E 8LU England

Printed in the United States of America

ISBN (Perfect): 0-8191-3744-8
ISBN (Cloth): 0-8191-3743-X

All University Press of America books are produced on acid-free
paper which exceeds the minimum standards set by the National
Historical Publications and Records Commission.

To

Maria and

Karl Voigt

ACKNOWLEDGEMENTS

We are, of course, indebted to a prestigious legacy of social thought. There are several individuals, however, who deserve sincere gratitude for their critical comment and support of this book. To Severyn Bruyn, David Horton Smith and Benedict Alper, all from Boston College, a special word of thanks is in order for their insightful commentary and insistence to clarify concepts. We also want to acknowledge the support of the Loyola University Grants Committee which financed a major portion of the production of this book. To Evangeline Mann a special word of thanks is given for her expert typing and editing. Finally, we offer a word of appreciation to our families whose self-sacrifice and whose support cannot be understated.

THE LIMITS OF JUSTICE: A SOCIOLOGICAL ANALYSIS

Table of Contents

Table of Contents

List of Tables

Chapter One

THE SOCIOLOGICAL SIGNIFICANCE OF JUSTICE

The question of justice generally emerges as a problem of meaning. The issue of justice frequently predicts a society within which its meaning is as intensely denounced by some as it is fervently held by others. It provides, on the one hand, arguments for the maintenance of the status-quo, and propounds, on the other hand, dreams and schemes of future utopias. Historically, the meaning of justice has been complicated by a context in which traditional systems of certainty are crossed by doubts and misgivings, while new systems and programs are broken by multilateral strains, and monistic persuasions are invaded by an ironic relativism.

The questions "What is justice?" or "What are the ways of attaining justice?" are not simple ones, nor are they new. Indeed, the concept is represented both by an impressive and respected intellectual heritage, and an enormously confused legacy of definitions.

Most critics of the concept of justice complain that its content is essentially enigmatic, and its structure indeterminate. The implication often being that the concept of justice is a sterile philosophical abstraction, serving as nothing more than an intellectual pastime. Accordingly, justice is believed to be devoid of both explanatory and pragmatic significance, in the sense, that it does not convey anything concrete.

Individuals and societies are dynamic, and their goals impart themselves in differing terms, and with varying degrees of urgency. The quest for justice does not take place under utopian or artificially simplified conditions, but amid the uncertain welter and flux of reality. The social fabric within which any particular mode of justice may be realized is neither universal nor altogether plastic. Depending on the specific nature of the orientation, justice imposes certain demands, limits, and directives. Super-imposed on this fundamental fact of variability is the subjectivity of human preference and cultural relativism. To complicate matters more, even when value preferences and social institutions are coordinated to motivate individuals in certain ways toward the attainment of a

1

particular resolution of justice, certain social circumstances may still influence differing verdicts regarding both the evaluation of ends and means, and their implication for future behavior.

The inextricable relationship between the variables of justice and the variables of human nature and social facts renders the impossibility of one universal definition of justice. Indeed, history demonstrates that no one formulation of justice has yet been proposed which is able to take into account human and social variables, so that it is both demonstratively free of value judgments and universally applicable or appropriate. For this reason, there is no effort made in these pages to expound a new theory of justice or to treat any one absolute formula of justice. Rather, the attention is directed to the question of what people actually mean when they ascribe the value of justice to an action or decision.

For example, if we accept that history has not produced any absolute formulation of justice, but represents many interpretations of its meaning, the taking account of the reasons one has for deciding in a particular fashion becomes particularly significant for a sociology of knowledge. The generalized concept of justice as a social variable cannot provide by itself any sociological use in research. But if justice can be progressively specified in its meaning as a social value so that it can be understood as a theoretical construct in the phenomenological tradition, justice can become an important sociological concept. By focusing on the reasons one has for deciding a certain way so that his/her actions are just, or by isolating the values which influence the reasoning behind certain decisions and actions of justice, or by linking these to theoretical systems; the purpose is to uncover the latent structure of justice in culture. Accordingly, the major problem in the sociological study of justice is to determine its latent structure.

We propose that the latent structure may be abstracted through a systematic study of the expression of justice in culture. The field of literature on justice is an important part (summative expression) of culture. The perception of the existence of justice as a concept of literature (e.g., philosophy, law) is the first step toward determining its essence or fundamental structure.

Once the latent structure of justice is identified, we can then apply it to the study of its social expressions in daily existence. The role of research then turns to revealing the expression of justice as a variable in particular institutions or social issues in order to more fully clarify their complex nature. Certain structural features of justice are emphasized, while others are missing at any given time in history. Thus, the application of this method leads to the discovery of a basic structure, which expresses certain constant elements as well as variations.

The dynamics of the decision-making process involved in the judgment of justice points to the relationship between the variable and the constant structure. Justice in terms of the decision-making process suggests the reintegration in the sociology of knowledge, aiming at being phenomenological, the whole of a vast field now outside it - a field which includes among other things the very method by which the sociology of knowledge is developed.

Some immediate questions can be asked: How is social knowledge grasped? How does sociological theory facilitate an awareness of it? Social reality has both subjective and objective components. Knowledge of society depends upon the processes of internalization, externalization and objectification which are dialectically interrelated (Berger and Luckmann, 1963). The dynamics involved in the social knowledge of such a concept as justice are the same as the dynamics involved in the social construction of reality. Justice exhibits both subjective and objective properties. In the first sense, the "essense" or "existence" of the question of justice which is raised in social life is determined by subjective factors, as for example, those involved in the case of a concrete controversy over justice. In the latter sense, the essence or existence of the issue of justice is culturally determined. What is of special interest is the correlation between the subjective and objective aspects of the various experiences associated with the concept of justice.

The sociology of knowledge invites us to discover how reason is shaped by social factors. The "sociological imagination" suggests that the social function of reason is to "formulate choices to enlarge the scope of human decisions in the making of history" (Berger and Luckmann, 1966). Accordingly, the conceptual scheme of justice introduced here provides a method whereby the growth of reason and the formulation of choices within changing and conflicting social structures may be studied. This may deepen our comprehension of how values function in social institutions and the sources of conflict inherent in them. In this respect, phenomenological analysis can serve to facilitate social analysis. Moreover, the conceptual system developed from this method may provide the basis for new propositions and theory. The new propositions and theory may be developed around the notion of the hidden dimensions of justice, and how these dimensions may be expressed in the future. For example, one proposition is that a state of disequilibrium prevails until all elements are somehow accounted for or expressed together. A

3

corollary is that the suppression of any single feature of justice may suggest that we can anticipate change that leads towards its ultimate expression. In this sense, the sociological treatment of justice may offer the broader goal of predicting some major social trends, particularly those that constitute the basis of social change.

A sociological treatment of justice may not only lead to the understanding of the context of the acting out of justice; but it is also a means for the study of the influence of justice ideas on the social structure. The concept of justice may occupy a particularly important place in sociology; since, it represents an integral part of human activity and human institutions.

The present treatment of justice is not without precedent in sociology. Vilfredo Pareto (1935) for example, examined literature systematically to determine the residues or constant elements which underlie human motivation. Pitirim Sorokin (1937-1941) studied the history of culture to determine how the structure of truth (ultimate criteria: reason, sense, faith) is expressed in its variations. And Talcott Parsons (1951) abstracted a set of universal dilemmas of orientation (pattern variables) which must be resolved before any action can take place.

In a similar tradition, we argue, that any account of what constitutes justice depends on an examination of the fundamental structure of meaning and values. This structure may, then, be employed to pick out factors of general relevance to certain decisions or actions concerning justice in culture. The structure is both objective and subjective. It is objective to the extent that there is agreement over its existence, and in the sense of, expressing some constant elements. It is subjective to the extent that it underlies certain specific actions or decisions and expresses variability. Both the subjective and objective qualities are vital to our understanding of the concept. Since the constant elements are necessary, but not sufficient to the understanding of the concept of justice, any attempts to solve the whole problem of the controversy over justice in history cannot be rationally approached by searching for merely the constant aspect of its meaning. The influence of cultures are, thus, essential to the historical significance of justice. It is on this ground, that the concept of justice has distinct implications for sociology.

While justice appears overwhelmingly variable, upon closer examination, it tends to reveal certain basic recurring value themes. Once the fundamental themes can be identified, we may uncover the underlying social values associated with them; and, then, study their variable expression in the conflict of

4

interests within society. Attention will be given to the constant thought structures of justice, and their relationship to the development of the idea of justice in history; and the mutable substance of meaning as well, and its relationship to the history of justice and the innovation of justice ideas.

The literature is "content-analyzed" both (1) thematically and (2) semantically. Once certain fundamental themes are intuitively abstracted, they are tested against the literature. Then, following the dictates of the literature, these themes are generally defined. The next step involves deriving a common vocabulary which is typically associated with the basic types of delineations of the "essence" of justice, noting the frequency with which certain terms are connected with certain themes.

The methodology considered for the analysis of the constitutional elements of justice and the essential permanent structure is also used to indicate the variety of ways in which the fundamental contexts of justice may be linked to reality. This link is intended to bridge the gap between the "essence" or the abstract elements of justice as grasped in the consciousness of the writers on justice, and the "existence" or the social phenomenal expression of justice in social problems.

The sources, development and organization of the social knowledge of justice, especially the expression of certain fundamental patterns of interpretation within social systems, all warrant sociological inspection. It is doubtful that any one particular method of approach or theoretical paradigm will be sufficient to capture the full social implications of such a concept as justice. The present endeavor represents only one way this problem may be approached. It serves only to point out that the concept has a significant sociological potential, which must be explored further.

The traditionally philosophical concept of justice need not be discarded from sociological consideration merely on the ground that it is subjective and culturally variable. It is a concept which in spite of its variability persists throughout history. Its variability and constant persistence have substantial implications for the sociology of knowledge. Perhaps the intrinsic flexibility of its meaning allows justice never to lose its relevancy, and to embrace the whole spectrum of society including such issues as the quality of life, abortion, capital punishment, the venality among public officials, women's rights, minority oppression, quality education, urban violence, the legal system, and the conflict of social and private interests, and world conflict to name a few. Justice is not only a broad or abstract social concept representing consensus, it is an integral part of competition and conflict in society. Unless we take into account the scope of the role of justice in social action and its role in the creation and mitigation of conflict, the study of society will be incomplete. Justice is part of the process of ordering different values and human experience and of documentation of the nature of agreement and disagreement over certain values in history.

Chapter Two

THE SOCIOLOGICAL STUDY OF JUSTICE

The real importance of the concept of justice lies not in any absolute formulation but in its function as a social value. Indeed justice as a cultural value has been far too much neglected, expecially by sociologists.

A. Defining Justice Conceptually

An ontological definition of a social value is generally problematic because its specification usually consists of statements, which suggest a logical equivalence between the conceptual structure and some typical social expression of the value. A definition, in this sense, cannot accommodate fine nuances of meaning; it cannot explain the process by which the conceptual meaning may be altered as a result of different interpretations; and it cannot even account for the impact of the dynamics of scrutiny. Since social values exhibit many expressions in various institutional or social contexts, a static definition is ultimately rendered irrelevant and useless. Consequently, there must be an attempt made to establish the relationship between the ontological nature of a value concept and its concrete referent in society.

From this perspective, the concept of justice is especially difficult to grasp. Justice appears to have an ontological reality, yet its definitional forms seem to have no phenomenal reality. History proves that the objectification of the concept of justice cannot be comprehended solely on the basis of its ontological meaning. Therefore, it is necessary to consider some method of studying the conscious correlates of the ways justice is ideally construed and the ways justice is culturally expressed. In other words, the problem is to understand the relationship between the connotative (idealistic) and the denotative (realistic) meaning of justice. The assumption here is that social knowledge is an interrelated combination of both connotative and denotative meaning.

A connotative meaning of justice suggests what a situation which is labeled "just" represents, and what individuals ideally mean when they say something is just. Emphasis is placed on the conceptual or grammatical significance of justice. Denotative meaning, however, embraces the sociological and psychological context surrounding what is labeled as justice. While the connotative definition of justice is essentially abstract and suggests an ideal situation or what might be in the future; the denotative definition is empirical in nature and implies what the situation was in the past or what it is in the present.

The concept of justice is especially interesting because its meaning seems to depend on the inherent inconsistency between the conception and the expression of justice, between what the word means to individuals and what they label as just in everyday life.

Plato, in the Republic (1892), the first great book on the subject of justice, suggests that no attempts to debunk the notion of justice by exposing the value-relativism of the various formulations of justice, can undermine its connotative essence. Socrates states that even when the interpretation of what is just depends heavily on the interests of the stronger, most people do not really intend this when "justice" is semantically selected for use. Plato insists that we must not limit the use of the concept to a mere labeling function; rather, we must become aware of the essential grammatical significance of justice. This includes an examination of the variety of occasions which determine that a particular situation or individual is just. Furthermore, justice cannot be comprehended merely by looking at the things which are considered just or at the individuals employing the term. Its meaning can only flow from what a situation symbolically represents when it is called "just," and what individuals are actually saying when they employ the word "justice" descriptively.[1] In this manner, Plato actually suggests how cultural-relativism can be minimized: given that the idea of justice may be used in similar language patterns in different cultures, it will have similar meanings despite the fact that the specific contexts or examples do not correspond.

Socrates can only grapple with the problem of justice by considering the ideal state, thereby, considering the virture of justice without its specific contextual implications. He reasons that justice is a fundamental constitutive value of social organization, which influences decisions and regulates political action. Socrates eventually derives three criteria elements of justice, contending that justice is an ideal, it is evaluative and it is prescriptive in nature.[2] As an ideal, justice is associated with certain other values; these values form the criteria for action. The evaluative component is expressed in terms of a "positive" assessment of an action or decision which constitutes

8

justice. Grammatically, then, justice suggests approbation. Finally, the prescriptive aspect takes the form of obligation, implying that individuals in comparable future situations must act similarly.

In Plato's metaphysical approach, the function of social values is the key to a basic understanding of the cognitive configuration of the consciousness of various definitions of justice. The various definitions which are based on different value premises give rise to our knowledge of justice in some grammatical, general or ideal sense. Plato appears to use the derivation of the concept of justice to illustrate the process of acquiring social knowledge. Consequently, he is implying that the differences and the contrariety of norms and values within and between societies are linked to the metaphysical question of the acquisition of knowledge. In this sense, Plato's fundamental problem concerning the meaning of justice is the acquisition of social knowledge.[3] Many social scientists agree that there are three basic features common to all value phenomena: (1) Values provide standards or criteria for decisions or actions. In this sense, they bring attention to various associative values or interest areas, connotating preference and emphasis. (2) Values enter into the process of rating objects, hence, demonstrating the evaluative component. However, values always imply a positive judgment or an approbative quality. In other words, things that are valued are considered good by virtue of being values. Values serve to distinguish what sorts of norms or phenomena are acceptable; and, therefore, they indirectly indicate what sorts of things are rejected. (3) Finally, values impute a directional component. They carry with them an implicit premise which serves as a referent for future behavior; and, to this degree, they illustrate the obligatory or prescriptive element.[4]

By treating justice as a value concept, the many definitions of justice may be transformed from competing alternatives into indicators of the general kinds of phenomena that are involved in the mundane everyday attempts to work out the problem of justice. It is unlikely that the concept of justice is apprehended on the basis of only one isolated experience. It is equally unlikely that the process of awareness of justice is predicated on associating one value at a time with its meaning. Quite the contrary, there appears to be a great interdependence between the value of justice and other values. For example, in one area of society justice may be typically expressed in terms of the law; while in another, its meaning may be related to the value of equality or freedom.

Therefore, the specific definitions of justice suggest the ways in which people try to organize and develop uniformity in their social lives. To this end, the concept of justice reflects

9

certain patterns of values that people use as general guidelines for their own actions, for judging the actions of others, and for indicating the direction of future actions. To be socially relevant, justice has a unique dependence on the recurrence of certain patterns, consistency among values, and the ability to be generalized. Thus, justice in the sense of expected value sets provides the basis for the claims and duties of individuals and societies. The acceptance of any particular cultural definition of justice rests on the common associative values established by culture and on the degree of social solidarity which reinforces the values within that culture.

By understanding justice as a social value, reference is made to a general rather than a particular system of criteria, which are formed independent of a specific individual's wishes. It refers to values or sets of values which remain relatively constant over time and which reflect and transcend specific cultural influences. This is not to say that personal wishes do not influence the conceptualization of justice or how the values and their inter-connectedness are interpreted, nor is it to say that the ideas of justice are beyond cultural relativism. What is implied here is that justice, when considered in the sense of a social value, may be studied in terms of some objective requirements. The consideration of justice as a value concept opens the way from studying it from a sociological perspective.

The three criteria elements which the concept of justice and other value concepts share (i.e., ideation, evaluation, and prescription) serve to amplify the fundamental problematic in justice. They suggest the main reason why the search for an absolute meaning of justice turns out to be such an onerous and impossible task.

Justice, as an ideal or standard, is supposed as a condition and is expressed, in some sense, in all societies. However, the specific norms or values which constitute the ideal are determined by agreement and thus vary from culture to culture. Its dependence on cultural consensus constitutes one aspect of the problematic in justice.

While justice exhibits an evaluative component, it is important to note that an assessment in terms of justice is approbative. Justice is an expression of what is considered "good" in culture. But the questions of how and why the evaluative component indicates approval or good is another problematic in justice.

Finally, the prescriptive element in the concept of justice implies that judging a certain course of action or decision as "just" obliges comparable actions or decisions in future situations. This prescriptive quality of justice, however, of how and why it obligates individual or social future action, constitutes another basic problematic in the concept.

Several crucial questions steming from the criteria elements, and the inherent problematic associated with them may form the basis for a study of justice in culture. (In other words, they may comprise the initial variable list for content analysis). First, what are some of the associative values which influence individual action or institutional expression? How are they represented in the various formulations of justice? How are actions measured and amalgamated into a judgment of just and unjust?

We assert that the three criteria elements of justice can serve as a fact-controlled frame of reference by which an understanding of justice as a social process of valuation may be approached. It is assumed here, that any formulation of justice must at least implicitly take into account these three fundamental elements, and somehow deal with the problematic associated with them. Noting the many ways in which these elements are expressed in the theories of justice throughout history will constitute the first stage of our sociological analysis of the justice as a cultural value.

Justice may be of particular importance for the sociology of knowledge, from the point of view that the study of justice may provide the unique opportunity for observing the dynamic interaction between the atemporal absolute prerequisites underlying the function of values in society, and those dimensions of symbolic meaning which allow a society to generate for itself novel and more complex systematic modes of adjustment. Accordingly, by having an appreciation for both connotative and denotative meanings of justice, we can take into account in the present something that is expected in the future. Thus, the social knowledge linkages of the past and future to the present may become apparent by looking at the relationship between the connotative and the denotative definitions of value concepts.

The development of the concept of justice historically is not the product of pure chance; rather, it represents an intelligible progression of thought. The innovative ideas of justice are not accidental either; they are part of the very nature of the process of conceptualization and of the working out of justice in everyday life. Regardless of the degree of success which a society or social institution claims in establishing common values and norms relevant to justice, these are never totally apprehended mentally or accepted by everyone in the society. Some individuals or groups will always demonstrate some degree of autonomy or some creative ability with respect to their value performance and conceptual

11

understanding of institutions. For instance, people express many unique responses or attitudes toward the norms or values of certain institutional expressions of justice.

With the overall acceptance of the interrelatedness of social facts and ideas in the formation of social knowledge, an even more basic assumption is necessary. In order that we may assume the interrelatedness of experiences and ideas, we must accept the possibility of a concrete method of discriminating between the empirical experiences and thought structures pertaining to concepts. The possibility of this latter assumption would render the sociology of knowledge futile. Thus, assuming that the distinction is within the realm of consideration, the following question must be posed: How can justice be understood both conceptually and culturally (or sub-culturally)?

B. Data, Sampling and Methodology for the Study of Justice

The phenomenal data which provides the basis for the present inquiry are the statements by many authors, who from their individual and collective experiences of the nature of reality, have contributed to the conceptual system of justice. The question of whether these statements may be considered as constitutive of the nature of reality or as merely subjective interpretations or mental transformations of it, is perhaps among the most important. Even though it is probably true that everything which is empirical may be considered for sociological investigation, certain types of data may impose methodological limitations. Since the empirircal basis for this analysis is made up of the traces of thought on justice in the form of written records, the content of the data is subjective from at least two perspectives. Not only is the data subjective because it represents only a slice of the interaction between ideas and cultural experience; but it is also subjective because it is evaluated and transformed according to the mental processes of the investigators.

Although the facts are undoubtedly subjective, we can assume that they are guided by a special norm - the desire of each author to be objective in his/her particular contribution. The phenomenal data which comprise this research are made up of many different ideas of justice, which are themselves attempts at some sort of systemization. In this sense, the data may be regarded as fragments of cultural as well as conceptual systems.

12

This, of course, leads to the problem of sampling. The sample is composed of only the most influencial and most recognized theories of justice. In order to enable an analysis of how theories develop and how they influence or are influenced by other individual's ideas and experiences emphasis on the most "important" contributions is vital to the present treatment. By following the "important" works through history, we may begin to uncover the atemporal or transcendental ideas or values which are passed on from generation to generation or from one culture to another. It also suggests the nature of ideas or experiences which tend to be dropped from consideration because they may be conceptually irrelevant or too culturally bound.

It is the transformation or reinterpretation of certain persisting ideas or values which may provide the insight into the degree to which the constant elements of justice interact with social reality.[5]

The selection of the most reputable and substantial contributions to the concept of justice is based on the following criteria:

(1) The author must have written at least one book (or a portion of a book) or article devoted exclusively to a unique theoretical conception of justice - authors who merely provide a compendium of theories on the subject are not considered individually for their contribution - although their works may have been consulted for a greater appreciation of the historical trends. (Total number of authors: 319)

(2) A list is kept from the begining of the study, which notes the rate of references made to certain authors or particular contributions. Fifty two authors are selected from the present analysis since they are the most frequently mentioned among the authors. Each author in the sample has at least ten references by ten different authors representing different historical periods. Each of the sample author's contribution comprised the center of attention in at least one other theory (this is decided on the basis of the number of pages or cross references found in the index of the book). Or it is based on the author's own acknowledgement of this.

(3) There is also an attempt made to represent different historical periods - thus, even if an author is not noted for his/her individual contribution, but can be considered a link in the historical development of the justice concept, this author was included. (Number of authors: 12)

(4) In some instances there is an exception made to the above criteria. For example, an author may not have necessarily contributed an entire piece on justice, but because his/her ideas had a great impact on the intellectual development of justice, the author is included nonetheless. (Marx is a case in point). (Number of authors: 7)

Generally, when there is some doubt about the inclusion of some author, the decision is always in favor of inclusion. The effort is to be as comprehensive as possible.

In order to avoid the recreation of isolated or unique conceptual schemes, taken out of their historical context, we focused the examination on representative statements of certain positions which transcend time. Such a procedure leads to the surfacing of the basic presuppositions involved in certain trends of thought.

Since there are numerous contradictory views about the meaning and epistemological status of the concept of justice, we consider the derivation of theoretical constructs. The use of the theoretical construct (with a particular emphasis on the developmental characteristics of the concept over time) is intended to demonstrate a method of obtaining the objective relationship between the forms of thought on justice and their socio-historical context. The historical constructs (as they will be called) are developed by the intensification of the dominating themes of justice, throughout time, and by the synthesis of numerous discrete or diffuse ideas or experiences associated with them. These historical constructs are ordered with special ideas which are recurrent in the writing on justice. The ideas are organized in a unified analytical model.

A major task in the development of the historical constructs is an analysis and comparison of viewpoints, and the discovery of the focal concerns, including the issues of debate, the theoretical tradition, and the theoretical inadequacy, so that we may approximate with some degree of assurance a more general formulation of the problem. To this end, the purpose is to provide clarity and to ennumerate the issues involved in the investigation.

Inductive abstraction, in the sense Husserl (1970) intended, in combination with deductive abstraction, constitutes the basic approach taken to the development of the historical constructs. Induction has been acknowledged by sociologists (e.g., analytic induction) as a process of acquiring general knowledge about particular information or experience; it leads to the organization of knowledge; but deductive logic leads to the specification of the particulars of knowledge. As the contents of the historical constructs begin to take shape, intuitively, a constant empirical check against the literature representing different historical periods is carried on. This is done to prevent the exclusion of any major themes or ideas of justice, and to control for any selective bias. To accomplish the empirical check, a method of semantic analysis is devised: a running check list of terms which are associated with certain ideas of justice is kept, including a list of cognates and synonyms, which may serve in the connection of primary and derived concepts.

Indices of books on justice also provide a means by which to empirically check the thematic trends. Most books aim to impose some conceptual frame of reference. This structure is important because it indicates some of the primary presuppositions and some of the associative concepts. Assuming that there is some order to books, we may look to the number of cross-references in the index for an indication of their thematic content (i.e., the items carrying the greatest number of cross-references or the items which have the greatest number of pages devoted to them may be taken as indicative of the author's orientation or priorities). A close inspection of a book's index and table of contents, gives us information about the organization of the work. This technique is especially useful when there is some doubt about the classification of any particular theory. Since the systematic organization becomes apparent when we make a comparison of several indexes of books which share similar orientations, a categorization can be made quickly by use of this comparative method.

On the basis of an intuitive content analysis, and an empirical index analysis, three historical constructs of the concept of justice can be identified: (1) Normative Conformity; (2) Public Interest; and (3) Individual Autonomy. These terms, which are used to label the historical constructs, are intended to briefly express the central theme represented by each model. The three historical constructs may be described and compared in terms of the criteria elements of value concepts: ideation, evaluation and prescription (see Chapter Three). Each historical construct provides a unique set of answers to the questions of ideation, evaluation and prescription. Therefore, the content of each construct represents a unique logical sequence of ideas and assumptions.

15

They represent a unique relationship to different theoretical traditions, including the emphasis on the specific theoretical problems or bias, and the complications of each tradition which is connected developmentally with each construct. Each basic type of formulation of justice not only relates to a unique aspect of reality or culture, but it also provides a referent to certain qualities which transcend that context and enables it to persist. In addition to the apparent intuitive thematic differences, the index analysis implies that each historical construct may be identified according to a unique vocabulary, some of which changes and some of which is relatively constant. The distinction of the unique value themes with their corresponding vocabularies provides the basis for the development of indicators through which the variable of justice can be compared and analyzed. The comparative technique involves uncovering the fundamental types of value orientations and verbal expressions which constitute the fundamental thought structures of justice. Accordingly, it is assumed, here, that the constructs may be associated with the conceptual formation and the structures through which the concept functions and changes.

Another methodological question comes to the forefront: the extent to which the inductive and empirical abstractions (including the isolation of the associative verbal as well as the related conceptual expressions of justice) are relevant when separated from their sociohistorical context. First, we must consider the problem of inclusiveness. Essentially, a theoretical "factor analysis" of the writing on justice, involving an extensive examination of their corresponding indices, is performed. Based on this analysis, an open code is derived, allowing for the inclusion of any thematic trends or modes of expressions in the literature on justice. There appears to be substantial evidence, however, in the literature, to support the existence of three themes or schemes of thought on justice.

Internal proof of the inclusiveness and representativeness of the historical constructs consists of indicating the manner in which these constructs function to organize the detailed data of the various interpretations or systems of justice throughout its intellectual history. External proof may be evident in the ability of developing from the historical constructs a summary set of conceptual dimensions which constitute the overall meaning of justice. The set of conceptual dimensions (see Chapter Four) must be able to subsume the unique contributions as well as the shared characteristics of the three historical constructs. The development of the conceptual dimensions are important to the extent to which it is possible to specify the conditions of the change or transformation evident in the development of the concept of justice historically.

The conceptual dimensions which are developed from the literature on justice represent sets of values or ideas which are typically associated with the concept of justice (e.g., equality, impartiality, law, etc.). Their derivation consists of isolating the most recurrent themes in the literature. Again, given the variability in treatments a generalized categorization or system is devised. The derivation of the conceptual dimensions includes a consideration of the process of decision-making which is involved in a judgment of just or unjust.

The system of conceptual dimensions suggests that the concept of justice necessitates making decisions among various associative values. The inherent complexities and contradictions in justice are made apparent through the system of conceptual dimensions. The acceptance of certain definitions of values involves making a decision among other alternative definitions. The decision-making process also includes the acceptance of some values as associative and the rejection of others as irrelevant.

Because a decision necessitates the selection of one among several alternatives, it inevitably entails forsaking the attractive features of the rejected alternatives and accepting the negative features of the chosen alternatives. By definition, every decision is followed by the dissonance process.

Since justice involves making decisions among associative values, it, too, is subject to post-decisional effects. A particular theory of justice may itself represent a mode of reducing cognitive dissonance, since most theories seem to go through the steps of minimizing the importance of other sets of alternatives or other positions, and accentuating or maximizing those which are accepted. Therefore, by concentrating on the controversy surrounding the concept of justice, we may begin to unearth the range of associative values or conceptual dimensions connected with justice.

In order to follow the controversy historically, it is imperative to focus only on the most important conceptual dimensions. Importance is defined in terms of (1) persistence over time; (2) prevelance; (3) degree of emphasis given by different authors, and (4) applicability to all historical constructs.

The set of conceptual dimensions is presented in terms of dichotomous variables which are generally defined in such a manner that they may subsume other ideas but cannot themselves be subsumed by any other ideas or systems. The conceptual dimensions include the following pairs of alternatives: sameness/diversity; interpersonal subjectivity/impersonal objectivity; improvement/stability; other-

17

consciousness/inner-consciousness;   perfectionism/practicality; and sanctioned duty/private duty.

The system of the conceptual dimensions is objectively real to the degree that it is logically prior to the subjective decision-making process involved in a judgment of justice. A decision is logical to the extent that it is in agreement or identical with the objective conceptual scheme. Following, there are two methodological problems involved in the development of the conceptual dimensions: (1) the problem of inclusiveness, and (2) the problem of fit or congruence.

The first test of the question of inclusiveness is whether the dimensions actually intuitively communicate the information necessary for understanding the meaning of justice? Second, to what degree do the dimensions specify the conditions of change in the development of justice? Third, to what extent can they explain the internal dynamics of the conceptualization of justice and the conditions of its development and continuity?

The problem of fit or congruence is raised when the conceptual dimensions are applied to the historical constructs. Each historical construct shares two alternatives with each of the other constructs, and each expresses two unique alternatives. Consequently, each construct is represented by a distinctive pattern of conceptual dimensions. The Normative Conformity construct of justice includes: sameness, impersonal objectivity, stability, other consciousness, practicality and sanctioned duty. The Public Interest construct of justice suggests: diversity, impersonal subjectivity, improvement, other consciousness, practicality, and private duty. Finally the Individual Autonomy construct of justice expresses: sameness, impersonal objectivity, improvement, inner consciousness, perfectionism, and private duty. The question of fit pertains to those theories which do not fit any one of the systems or constructs. It is believed, here, that individual thinkers on justice do not address their total society nor do they respond to the entire range of social reality. Instead they select certain publics or segments of society as objects of their concern (Znaniecki, 1940). Other problems of fit and questions of general consistency are discussed in Chapter Four.

From a phenomenological perspective it is the purpose of Chapter Four to demonstrate that the conceptualization of justice is not just a process of meaning, but also a process of continuous organization of experience (i.e., linking the "essence" of justice with the "experience" of justice). Subsequently, the decision-making process involved in the conceptualization of justice gives way to response acquisition, with special attention to combination and recombination of value responses and stimuli. Thus, the conceptualization of justice

18

may be viewed as a process of continuous crystallization of different types of values, which regulate social interaction in times of conflict of interests. Finally, the defining characteristics of the consciousness of justice, in the ordinary sense of that term, consists of the fact that justice is the consciousness of certain values.

Chapter Five seeks to demonstrate that once the latent structure of justice and its dimensions are discovered, one can apply them to the study of everyday life. The abortion controversy is used to illustrate the application of the conceptual scheme and to show how the concept of justice may be expressed in concrete social problems. A thorough literature search is conducted. Again, only the most important works are considered in the analysis. (The same set of selective criteria, including the concern for representativeness, which is applied above, is relevant here).

The definition of each conceptual dimension provides the basis for the content analysis of the issues of the abortion controversy. Accordingly, the fundamental positions within the abortion controversy are presented in relation to the patterns of the conceptual dimensions of justice. The treatment suggests that conceptually, the issue of justice in the abortion debate is similar to the issue of justice in general. The fact that the abortion dilemma is revealatory of the thought structures characteristics of justice, implies that the conceptual scheme may be employed to distinguish the objective issues and the subjective nature of responses surrounding the controversy. By treating the expression of justice as a variable in the organization of response to social problems, the attempt is to understand the subjective nature of social reactions to social problems more clearly.

Some other brief examples are considered in Chapter Six, since the abortion controversy may be somehow unique in its expression of the basic justice themes. The book generally demonstrates that justice may be amendable for sociological treatment complying with the rigorous rules of the discipline and it suggests how the concept of justice can be used in sociological investigation. The main purpose of the book is to introduce a method for linking certain abstract ideas (e.g., justice) with concrete experiences (e.g., social problems, such as abortion) and for styding their interaction in the formation of social knowledge. The present book represents only a beginning step in the study and systematic specification of justice. We hope the work will inspire others to consider this significant concept further.

Chapter Three

THREE HISTORICAL CONSTRUCTS OF JUSTICE

The purpose of this chapter is to demonstrate, with the help of textual explication, the nature of the three fundamental themes found in the theoretical literature of justice. In order to enable maximum generality and breadth of application the basic themes are presented in the form of historical constructs.

Each theme appears to have survived in spite of the subjective interpretations or treatment by different theorists, and irrespective of social change or historical context. While each theme represents certain transcendental qualitites or constant variables which may be identified historically, each theme also represents certain mutable characteristics or inconstant variables which may be traced developmentally.

The fundamental themes are intuitively abstracted from a study of the recurrence of several patterns of thought and of systems of semantics associated with the concept of justice in the major writings of modern Western history.

While admitting some overlap and numerous variants, each historical construct may be considered generally implacable. Each historical construct suggests a unique set of values, assumptions and vocabulary which are relevant to the analysis of the concept of justice. Accordingly, each construct of justice offers different interpretations of justice in reference to the pronouncement of associated values; and each indicates certain related evaluating and motivating components, which are distinct and mutually exclusive.

Thus, it is proposed that the decision-making process involved in determining any specific choice of values or meaning associated with the concept of justice may be expressed in terms of any one of the historical constructs. Following, the idea of justice may be expressed according to any one of these formulations: (A) conforming to the established norms of society or the normative order; (B) acting for the general welfare of the society or for the social good; (C) respecting individual freedom or human dignity. The fundamental perspectives have been called Normative Conformity, Public Interest and Individual Autonomy, respectively.

The writers who have been considered in the development of each construct have come from a variety of disciplines; and they represent a variety of historical epochs. Only a few sample writers are presented in the discussions of the historical constructs. The individuals are selected because they are considered to best represent the different facets of the construct. An attempt is made to give one a sense of historical development. Furthermore, the description involves statements of the ways each criteria element (ideation, evaluation, and prescription) finds expression in different theories.

The three historical constructs of justice are not without their limitations. For example, the coming discussions do not represent a compendium of thought on justice relevant to each construct; nor do they provide comprehensive accounts of the works of each philosophical position. Often, only a small portion of a philosopher's work serves to illustrate certain lines of thought, which may be used to identify the work with a specific thematic trend. Accordingly, different theorists belonging to different philosophical traditions or disciplines are classified according to common themes found in their work. Hence, it must be re-emphasized that each generic formulation is not the property of any one theorist or school of thought. While the constructs represent a simplification of the pattern of thought on justice, they seek to cut through the welter of differences and disagreements to reach a minimum consensus.

The ongoing criticisms leveled against not only positions taken within a general perspective, but also against the positions of different perspectives are very important developmentally. It is through the body of criticism that we can observe the elements of tension in theory and in society. The ongoing emergence of the concept of justice is intimately connected to the ongoing controversy over justice. Indeed, through the critique of each fundamental outlook, and precisely in its inability to be expressed ideally in reality, a working model of the decision-making process involved in approaching just resolutions can be dialectically comprehended.

A. Normative Conformity

The Normative Conformity construct of justice represents those theories of justice which hold in common the idea that the established law or the social order provides the only determinate and objective basis for understanding justice. People who may be historically associated with this general persepctive include: J. Austin (1954), F. H. Bradley (1876),

22

Emile Brunner (1945), Sigmund Freud (1948; 1952), Edwin Garlan (1941), Georges Gurvitch (1971), Hammurabi (1976), Thomas Hobbes (1949), Hans Kelsen (1957), Niccolo Machiavelli (1908), Chaime Perelman (1967), Jean Piaget (1932), Alf Ross (1959), Charles Stevenson (1944), to name just a few.

These writers would probably agree that the ideal of justice, irrespective of how faithfully it is held or how well it is expressed by such "catch all" contexts as human freedom or social good, is of little use in a quest for a just solution to a particular problem, unless it is defined in terms of the concrete normative social order or law. Some would go so far as to state that without a formal system of law, justice is empirically inconceivable. Moreover, the social order does not only provide the whole essence of justice, but it serves to reflect the commonly held values, which constitute the phenomenal experience of justice.

The following corollary may be inferred: Justice is not only dependent upon the normative order, but is secondary to it. Rather than enlisting justice to judge the government of behavior, the controlling norms form the basis for a judgment of justice. Indeed, the normative order provides the part of reality of which justice refers. Without the establishment of the normative order, the administration of justice is not possible.

The general theme that government and laws are primary for a consciousness of justice finds support in a line of theorizing which has persisted over the ages. The Normative Conformity construct, as this theme will be referred to, will be traced through its development historically.

The main questions here are: (1) how are the values associated with government or laws actually linked to the concept of justice? And (2) how are they to be understood?

There appears to be the accepted belief that even in common usage "laws" appear fundamental to the concept of justice. For example, ancient and primative cultures may be seen as developmental antecedents to contemporary society, as subtle indicators of modes of behavior in both action and thought. Broadly speaking, in ancient and preliterate societies, justice is defined by laws which are "given" and held to be immutable. In its earliest form, the idea that law is a body of commands of the sovereign power in a politically organized socity, and justice resting ultimately on the expression of the commands, appears in a divinely ordained or divinely dictated body of rules, as in Hammurabi's Code. When-

Anu, the supreme, and Bel, the Lord of Heaven and earth, who fixes the destiny of the universe,

delighted the flesh of mankind by calling me, the
renowned prince, the god-fearing Hammurabi, to
establish justice in the earth, to destroy the wise
and the wicked, and to hold back the strong from
oppressing the feeble, to shine like the sun-god
upon black-headed men and to illuminate the land .
. . . . .[6]

(to quote Hammurabi's own words about himself at the head of
his famous codes), the Babylonian and surrounding peoples of
Asia Minor already possessed an elaborate system of courts and
customs, of decrees and enactments and notion of justice.

Hammurabi's justice is distinctly connected to the concept
of law. But most importantly, justice emanates from the
codification itself, the fact that the law is handed down for
eveyone to observe equally. Affirming this, Hammurabi called
himself "King of Justice" because he received the legal order of
his kingdom from the hands of Shamash (Luizpen, 1967: 48).
Accordingly, the search for justice is a major enterprise of law,
and an attempt to characterize justice is inseparably connected
with that which characterizes law. Therefore, law must preceed
justice.

A similar extrapolation may be made on another level. It
is generally regarded that the physical development of an
individual and the development of his/her mentality go hand in
hand with cultural evolution. In other words, the culture of a
people can be deduced as evidence of their stage of mental
evolution. To this end, child development studies are often
cited to introduce such information.

Piaget, for example, reports that children acquire their
first notion of justice from the ideas of duty and obedience to
the commands of adult authority, which leads him to assert that
what is just is first known as "what is imposed by law." Piaget
in The Moral Judgment of the Child (1962), develops his theory
of justice by studying how boys learn to play the game of
marbles. The game's rules are passed down from child to child
with no adult intervention. Piaget's study indicates that as the
children acquire maturity in the playing of the game, they
begin to develop ideas which they use to judge the original
game rules; and which they later use to implement various
alternatives to the rules to make the game better. Piaget calls
this process the acquisition of "the spirit of the game" (1962:
71).

He contends that this same process occurs in the
acquisition of a consciousness of justice. Children first acquire
the spirit of justice from the rules of society. With maturity,

the consciousness of rules is crystalized into a sense of justice, which can be used to judge the original rules of society.

Furthermore, the actual rules, themselves, do not necessarily influence the precise sense of justice even though they give rise to it. Piaget insists that the original rules of the game of marbles are such that one could expect "the spirit of the game" to be very conservative. Yet the rules are treated very flexibly by the boys. That is to say, if the rules by which a certain concept is learned are strict, giving no latitude for change, one would expect the concepts learned from them to be characterized similarly. Piaget demonstrates however, that this is not the case. In spite of the strict rules of the game, Piaget found that children are able to innovate – create and accept other rules – without damaging the "spirit of the game." Similarly, when children initially learn what is just from the existing institutions, they can use those same concepts to evaluate and change the institutions, without disrupting the continuity of the "spirit of the institution."

Language itself, is considered one of the purest examples of culture or social experience, particularly in its independence of intentional control. Linguistics provide support for the legality of justice. It is important to note that justice is sometimes a synonym for law or lawfulness. Justice is a legal term (jus meaning law). However, every translation posits some particular problems. For example, the English language has no pair of words which can be opposed to each other, to express the contrast as in Russian between the words zakon and provo, or in German between Gesetz and Recht. The former in each case and its equivalent stress the idea of law as a binding rule, referring to a particular law or statute. The latter means law in the general sense or the larger sense, with a capital L, connoting Right of Justice. It carries the suggestion that law is related to a system of principles and, not to a mere arbitrary enactment. In legal philosophy (especially in German Rectsphilosophie) it often imputes the idea of ethical "rightness." Sometimes this is used with the qualifying epithet "subjective" to signify "a right," moral or legal. The word for justice in Russian is Pravosudiye; and in German it is Gerectigkeit. In each instance it is the latter word for "law" which is the root word for justice.

In the philosophy of justice the association with law is perhaps as old as philosophical thought itself. Plato acknowledges a distinctly legal definition of justice. The mythology of antiquity of ancient Greece has interrelated law and justice into a natural, real, and complex super-structure often resting on a divine foundation. In times of crisis, when edicts of sacred law, which were administered and accepted in the past without questions, were somehow unable to deal with social problems, they became the object of debate. For example, during the Greek enlightenment of the fifth century B.C., the distinction between the "natural" order, corresponding to the "nature" of humankind and the "positive" or normative order, created by humankind is introduced. This distinction produces the very substance for the philosophical development of the Normative Conformity construction of justice.

The Normative Conformity construct suggests that while there is a tendency to describe justice in terms of laws as may be evidenced in cultural, human developmental and linguistic studies, the philosophical debate over the so-called objective superhuman standard of justice and the subjective nature of human reasoning reduces to the latter. Every appeal to an absolute or universal must be justified realistically apart from any super-human terms. This type of argument takes on real significance during the "Age of Reason."

The Normative Conformity construct, thus, has its roots in the rejection of all notions of justice based on some superhuman standards or ability to penetrate the hierachy of values in general. Furthermore, the positivism of the nineteenth century, with its denial of metaphysical and superhuman, helps to dissolve any idea of justice which is not based on the objective criterion of the law by proclaiming the relativity of all views of justice which do not reduce to legal terms. The idea of justice is trimmed down to the responsive cognition so that its consciousness coincides with the effective social organization.

The complete codification of law at the beginning of the nineteenth century was accompanied by an abundance of writing on justice based on the notion of the social order. After which there is a special emphasis in the literature for the demand of a system of law without contradiction in form, and without any value system, as such, as a criterion in substance. Of course, the writings of many theorists over a long period of time have contributed to this legal reduction of the concept of justice.

Traditionally, the Normative Conformity construct of justice in its formal development has its roots in the theories of positive law. Hobbes (1946) posits the most consistent attempt to trace the concept of justice to positive law, exclusively in its value as preserver of life and order. Writing in a time of religious and civil wars, Hobbes could hardly place the essence of humankind on a foundation of reason. Instead, he views the essential feature of human behavior as the striving for power. Such striving inevitably leads to a war of all against all, if the state is not founded as a power making vehicle for order. In Hobbes' view, only the state can guarantee the protective order to the individual by establishing law, and then only by

26

exercising the hightest and most unlimited power under all circumstances. In all instances, the citizen is to be prevented from disregarding state regulations, in spite of any alleged contradictions between the citizen and higher norms of order. Hence, the content of such regulations is of no real concern: everything which the law-giving organization regulates must be held just.

Hobbes explains that the setting up of an organized society involves the formation of rules, which everyone agrees upon. At this level, Hobbes contends that the system of rules constitutes justice. He implies that justice is a sociological fact which assures that rules underlie the smooth patterns of interaction in society. Following, order in society will determine the nature of inculcation of the rules (spirit of the order) in its members, and, simultaneously, the essence of justice. Hobbes is suggesting that the rules and the concept of justice become internalized. The result is an ultimately sociological phenomenon of incorporating valuation in the organization of society. Consequently, all individuals possess the socially inculcated feelings of obligation and approbation which are inherent in the idea of justice. They may not, however, be aware of the relationship between social order and justice, which is at the root of the explanation of the coordination of social interaction in society. In essence, one's obligation to act a certain way is reduced to the demands by the formal norms that the society has laid down for its own protection. Therefore, it is the precise specifications of the social order which determines the meaning of justice in a particular society.

If Hobbes is correct, this same process of identifying justice with the social order which leads to a consciousness of justice can be traced on the sub-cultural level. W. F. Whyte's study (1965) of street corner gangs in a slum neighborhood is an example of how justice develops from organization and solidarity. The gang's code enjoins them to help their friends, to refrain from harming them. An ideal of justice is developed only in application to the group from within; it does not apply to the outside social mileu. The sense of obligation in such a group stops short at the boundaries of the group. It is a sense which derives in the manner that Hobbes describes - from a feeling of mutual dependence in the face of a hostile world. What is important to note, here, is that in spite of sub-cultural relativism, a concept of justice can be objectively determined from the code or law which functions to establish social cohesion and social order.

Hobbes claims that humankind is naturally guided by greed. In a presocial state individuals are constantly in conflict with one another. But the conditions are such that the

27

individuals are relatively equal in strength. No individual is so weak as not to pose some measure of threat to others; and, conversely, none is so strong as to be above fear of all others. In these conditions, there are no laws, no rights, and there is no security. An individual's life is "solitary, poor, nasty, brutish and short" (1946: 82). A society is developed only when individuals accept the notion that their inner interests are best secured within an ordered social life. The egocentricity of the unsocialized child roughly corresponds to the egocentricity of the natural individual described by Hobbes. In this respect, it is not a case of ego-centric adults entering society, but ego-centric children growing into society. The common acceptance of rules as this type of justice suggests depends on an "other-consciousness" and the appreciation of the value of security.

In order to maintain a secure existence and peace, steps must be taken to safeguard the person's social life against the out-break of the natural expression of self-interest. To accomplish this a "power to keep them in awe and to direct their actions to the common benefit" must be instituted. Stating it differently, an individual originally lives in a state of nature, which, without a central unifying power, is tantamount to living in a state of war. Hence, "Man is a wolf unto man" (Hobbes, 1947: 82). Hobbes stipulates that the unifying power must be entrusted in the sovereign, who, only through an unquestioned authority, can guarantee security. Since the sovereign is not part of the compact, and, since all his/her acts are consented to in advance by the people, the sovereign is above the law. The sovereign maintains this position as long as he/she is able to extend to the community his/her protection. The dependence of justice upon the existence of a superior power is supported by the following counter-factual argument:

> If we could suppose a great multitude of men to consent in the observation of Justice . . . without a common power to keep them all in awe, we might as well suppose all mankind to do the same; and then there neither would be, nor need to be any civil government or commonwealth at all (Hobbes, 1947: 129-130).

Hobbes, of course, assumes the impossibility of the consequent to prove the absurdity of the antecedent. For him, it is only too obvious that individuals require government to order their relations with one another.

A more recent rendition of this legal formulation of justice has been advanced by Kelsen (1957), who agrees that the normative order of a society determines what is just and unjust:

A man is just if his behavior conforms to the norms of a social order supposed to be just (12).

In addition, Kelsen insists that law in itself, is independent of the idea of justice; and that justice cannot be the criterion of law. To ask the question, whether a law is just or unjust, is redundant; since, the question reduces to: "is law a law?" He argues that the question, "is law just," cannot be ascertained scientifically and is simply impractical (6). The reason for this is because every system of law assumes a justice which is relative to that law. It originates with the idea that the social order is the most practical criterion of its meaning.

What makes the general position expressed by the Normative Conformity construct special and distinct is precisely the notion that law or a constitution or a code suffices itself, independently, to provide a determinate and objective norm of justice. Moreover, what is even more significant in all this, is that by denying that justice supplies the criterion for law, it follows that justice is unable to function as a practical standard for legislators. However, as Kelsen succeeds in pointing out, justice, with respect to law, serves as a standard only for its execution and application, and not for its derivation as such.

Austin (1954), another theorist in this tradition, goes so far as to say that "law is itself a standard for justice" (24). Alf Ross (1959) also supports this orientation in his comparison of the activities of judges and legislators. He maintains, for instance, that justice functions as a criterion of the judge's activity. Ross writes:

> The words "just" and "unjust" . . . make sense when applied to characterize the decision that is made by a judge - or any other persons dealing with the application of a given set of rules. To say that the decision is just means that it has been made in regular fashion, that is, in conformity with the rule or system of rules in force (274).

For Ross, justice in terms of the formal normative order, may be distinguished from other formulations because the judge, who is the individual responsible for applying it, is not free to choose a personal conception of justice. The judge is bound to observe the established rules. In addition, Chaime Perelman (1963) concludes that "formal justice, then, simply comes down to the correct application of a rule" (39).

However, when the words just or unjust are used in reference to a legislator the situation changes. Ross (1959) insists:

Applied to characterize a general rule or order, the words "just" or "unjust" are entirely devoid of meaning. Justice is no guide for the legislator . . . Applied in this connection (i.e., with regard to the content of the rule or order), the words have no descriptive meaning at all (274).

In identifying justice with conformity to some formal system of normative order, one necessarily rejects any theory of natural right in humankind. It will be recalled that Hobbes (1947) insists that the quality of justice is not a natural quality in humans. He writes that:

Justice and injustice are none of the faculties neither of the body, nor of the mind. If they were they might be in a man that was alone in the world, as well as his senses and passions (152).

When individuals are utterly without norms, no questions of justice or injustice arises. When there is no government, there is no justice.

The tradition which Hobbes has influenced generally assumes that an individual cannot reach the perfection of his/her nature except in and through civil society and, therefore, that civil society is prior to the individual consciousness of justice. In this view the primary obligatory force in justice is sanctioned duty. The assumption is that we must be forced to act a certain way before we can choose to act that way. We cannot assert the primacy of natural rights without asserting that the individual is valued in every respect prior to civil society: according to this, all rights of civil society or of the sovereign are derivative from the value of human rights which originate within the individual consciousness of him/herself. Most writers who deal with justice in the Normative legal sense tend to deny the notion of natural law.

It is important, at this point, to turn to the question of how this basic legal approach views the specific content of other value systems connected with the concept of justice. First, the rejection of the value of human rights in the theory of justice can be understood in several ways. Emile Brunner's (1945) renunciation of a human-right in justice is expressed as follows:

'That is my due, that is your due,' simply means – it is so established, it is already determined. We have given the name of primal order to this foreordination of what is due. But where there is order, there is law. Hence the idea of Justice is inseparable from law (21).

Furthermore, Perelman explains that none of the theories espousing the notions of human right or freedom and social good have been successful in delineating the content of the "just order" in an objective and determinate manner. Similarly, Kelsen (1961) believes that the idea of "natural right" is founded on "self deception or what amounts to the same thing; it is an ideology" (8). With this, he means that a notion of justice resting on natural right cannot accommodate an objective system of norms on which justice may be grounded.

Freud (1948) also links justice to social order but his reasoning is unique. Freud begins by suggesting that traditionally the concept of justice is a myth. He asserts that it is an illusion, but an illusion which is grounded in a psychologically real dilemma. The illusion stems from the need to be loved. The organization of the individual ego, the family, and the society, all depend on the illusion that all the members share "equally" in the love of the father or the interest of the government, respectively. Regardless of the level of extrapolation "the same illusion holds good of there being a head - in the Catholic church, Christ; or in any army, its Commander-in-chief - in both cases the head supposedly loves all the individuals in the group with an equal love" (1948: 43).

In Totem and Taboo (1952), Freud explains how the demand for equal love is an inherent part of the process of identification. Siblings begin to view one another as friends and not rivals, only after they are made to realize that no one of them can win the love of the mother or nurse exclusively.

> The first demand made by this reaction - formation
> is for all . . . If one cannot be the favorite
> himself, at all events nobody else shall be favorite
> (86-87).

Accordingly, justice appears to rise out of ego frustration. Freud maintains that whatever the level of social organization, whether it be a nursery or a factory, the demand for justice is derived from a desire which begins with individual failures to attain total personal gratification; and which concludes in an unconscious pursuit to subject similar deprivation upon others. The quest, then, for social justice is rooted in an unconscious wish to impose an equality of frustration upon one's peers. Freud says:

> No one must want to put himself forward, everyone
> must be the same and have the same. Social justice
> means that we deny ourselves many things so that
> others may have to do without them as well . . .

This demand for equality is at the root of social conscience and the sense of duty (1952: 88).

Furthermore, apart from the psychological function of justice, as described above, Freud suggests that it also has a role in preserving the arrangement of the social structure. He stipulates that a society depends on two elements: (1) a structure based on domination; and (2) the process of identification. First, the social structure is based on an ineradicable inequality of individuals in their tendency to form two classes: followers and leaders. Psychologically, justice, through the process of identification, responds to the demand of the weak for sameness in treatment or consideration; which, under other circumstances poses a situation which would be threatening to the ego. Consequently, the illusion of justice or idea of justice, pacifies discontent and frustration. Freud's theory allows the conflicting desires for authority and egalitarianism to exist simultaneously by promoting psychological justice as a complement to actual inequality. In effect, then, Freud concludes that the inclination toward justice is correlated with the need for stability in society.

The dimension of stability is not to be taken to mean static stability representing merely the maintenance of the status quo. The association of stability with justice includes the elements of change (recall Piaget's "Spirit of the game"). Specifically, when regarding "what ought to be," the concept of justice from a Normative Conformity perspective presses for a recognition of change. Justice expresses a temporal dimension, which is represented by the numerous directions and tendencies of history. The laws by which an individual judges specific actions and disputes are constantly in the process of development. Justice is a combination of movement and change, as well as permanence and structure.

If justice derives only from obeying the dictates of authority, and if the consciousness of justice can only emanate from the formal normative order, then, what is the real significance for a conceptualization of justice? If one assumes that the only rational and objective approach to a concept of justice is expressed in the idea of normative conformity, what is the need of such terms as justice and its derivatives: just or unjust?

Most apparent supporters of a Normative Conformity approach to the concept of justice would probably acknowledge, if only implicitly, that something would be conceptually missing if justice did not exist as an idea. To refer to an action as just implies something more than that it is legal or that the action supports the social order.

32

First, the evaluative component helps to differentiate justice from law, giving it special meaning. Stevenson (1944) for example writes that the concept of justice is necessary because it possesses both "descriptive" and "emotive" characterizations. It is descriptive because it expresses conformity/deviance or legal/non-legal relationships; and it is emotive because it implies good/bad or acceptable/non-acceptable.

The Normative Conformity construct posits a meaning of justice with both objective and subjective implications concurrently. It is suggestive of both norms and values at the same time. As a general norm of social action, it may be objectively derived. As a value it specifically implies what action is considered good by society (e.g., if it is legal, it is good). The Normative Conformity construct is unique in the attempt on the part of the authors to identify both subjective and objective characteristics. It is the only construct which provides a distinct explanation of both qualitites.

Secondly, justice is distinct from legality since it specifically carries a prescriptive connotation. The Normative Conformity orientation "how and why does justice prescribe behavior?" involves the following progression: Initially, since justice is defined in terms of law or norms, it has the implicit and explicit force of law or norms behind it (punitive might). This conception of justice not only incorporates the subjective positive evaluatory component, it also implies the pressure of the sanction of personal approval. Next, obligation and certain sets of expectations for behavior derive from the idea of the nature of ths social order. An individual is expected or required to behave according to the specifications of the social order because, otherwise, "destruction" and "disharmony" of the given "social system" may result. Furthermore, certain modes of expectations are anticipated simply by the conjectured acceptance of the social order. An individual acts according to the specifications of the social order, because it is approved; and, therefore, a concept of justice on this basis reinforces the accepted pattern of interaction between two or more persons.

In summary, justice according to the Normative Conformity construct may be described as follows: Its objectivity is based on the common acceptance of the value of norms or laws. It is predicated on conformity to norms and laws and on the interaction based on them. Justice is itself distinguished from laws or norms because it specifically carries an evaluatory component, which suggests that when an individual contends that an action is just, it is an accepted norm. Moreover, justice is prescriptive to the extent to which the normative and legal sanctions are established and

33

communicated in society. It does not depend on any inner notion of morality, rather it rests entirely upon the subjective agreement and common acceptance of the social order. The objective might of the society to enforce compliance with its organization constitute the primary obligatory forces. Most writers who approach this basic position would probably agree that positive law, and, consequently, the concept of justice, serve not only the functions of reflecting and conserving an antecedent order, but also those of depicting and realizing a prospective order. If justice is to be conceived of adequately, we must think of it as a creative agent that works between the poles of the actual and ideal; because, it is precisely this incompleteness and openness of the human milieu that determines the conceptual value of justice.

An over emphasis, however, on the social order in the definition of justice, may conceivably present some negative or undesirable results or anti-utopian ramifications. For example, there is the criticism that the use of a normative sense of justice cannot adequately serve as a device of organized social action directed toward achieving improvement in the social structure. The normative definition of justice often tends to ignore the real tension between the ideology of law (which tends to regard law as the stable foundation of social order) and the instrumental orientation of law (which regards the utilization of law as a means of social action). This may explain why there is relatively little attention given to the crucial question of the process of legal justification.

The fear is that politics or institutions which aspire to a definition of justice implied in the Normative Conformity construct may, in their anti-utopian form, place an unwarranted or unrealistic emphasis on the mystical guarantees of stability. In this context, justice means obeying mores, laws in minute particulars, even where they may be mere social conventions. As over emphasis on a loyality to convention may evolve into nothing but conformism, and may become especially alienating to future generations for whom the derivation of the conventions may be meaningless, in light of their new problems and needs. As stability becomes a moral force, it may also become the rationalizing agent for a repressive social order or social stagnation.

Of course, those who focus on the Normative Conformity definition do not usually deal with the negative aspects of their position. For those approaching this basic formulation, the main concern is the attributes of the conceptual scheme. The general feeling among these writers is that the old dream that law will wither away, has proved nugatory. Even Marcuse (1958) is forced to admit that justice, based on "the rule of law, no matter how restricted, is still infinitely safer than the rule above or without law."

But the crux of the matter is that even justice based on positive law does <u>not</u> guarantee humanity (i.e., good laws do not necessarily in<u>dicate</u> good human beings). Advocates of justice, in the sense of Normative Conformity, appear to delineate "matter of fact" humanity, "matter of fact" order and "matter of fact" peace. Justice, as Normative Conformity, may appear so fascinated by the undeniable importance of the normative or social order for the attainment of humanity, that it simply ignores the basis of justification (i.e., the critical value of that order).

B. Public Interest

The Public Interest construct relies on the notion of social good for its criterion of justice. While the notion of social good is variously expressed in the literature, most ideas of justice relying on social good are conceived in the sense of maximizing the expression of rights or interests in a pluralistic society. In order to allow the maximum expression of competing interests or coexistence of conflicting value systems, a partial surrender of individual freedom for the benefit of all is involved.

The theorists who generally espouse a Public Interest conception of justice reject the notion that justice may be reduced to the function of the normative order or law. Indeed, it is usually suggested that the concept of justice, in the sense of social good, may serve to evaluate the objective indicators of the social order. The mere association of certain laws with the label of injustice also implies that the laws are bad and that the social order may be in need of reform. Furthermore, the emphasis on individual freedom as the basis for the meaning of justice is also rejected, but the rejection is primarily on the grounds that the mere concern for the individual interest is basically contrary to the idea of social harmony. It is only through giving up some personal freedom that the general freedom of the entire society can be assured.

Among the individuals who may be fitted to a Public Interest construction of justice are the following: Aristotle (1965; 1967; 1891), R. W. Baldwin (1966), Arnold Brecht (1954), Jeremy Bentham (1961), Cardoza (1924), P. De Tourtoulon (1922), Leon Duguit (1918), Torstein Eckhoff (1974), Morris Ginsberg (1963), George Homans (1961; 1974), Leonard Hobhouse (1949), David Hume (1894), Rudolf Ihering

(1913), J. Kohler (1914), John Stuart Mill (1957), Clarence Morris (1963), F. A. Olafson (1961), Vildredo Pareto (1935), J. P. Plamenatz (1968), Roscoe Pound (1922; 1968), Pierre Proudhon (1876), John Rawls (1958, 1963, 1971), Nicholas Rescher (1966), H. Sidgwick (1962) and Rudolf Stammler (1925). Most these writers imply that social solidarity (with the resultant increase in the identification with a collective) provides the rudimentary basis for the conception of justice. The model calls for a perpetual pursuit of social welfare, with constant adjustment and mutual concession. Traditionally, this position has been considered in the context of the concept of social utility.

Contradicting the Hobbesian notion that "man is a wolf unto man," most proponents of a Public Interest perspective of justice would probably support an idea of natural justice. By this we mean that some semblance of social organization, and a basic consciousness of justice are believed to exist prior to any system of government.

For Aristotle (1887-1902), justice generally provides a natural criterion of goodness for both society and law. According to him, constitutions and laws may exhibit good or bad qualities, and may be just or unjust. He suggests that they can actually be measured in relation to their approximation of natural justice. Aristotle writes that the best state is the one most natural where "Men ... are just absolutely and not according to some particular standard" (8). The most important instance of the naturally just, in the Aristotelian sense, is the notion that equals should be treated equally. He declares that individuals as equal beings deserve to be treated equally; but, because people are also not identical, an arithmetic equality is inappropriate for a conception of justice. On this basis, he recommends that a state constitution take account of the differential principle under the general scheme of justice; that is, take into account a proportional equality (2). He goes on to stipulate that the constitution must not only express a standard for distribution, but that this standard must be based on the characteristics of society. In an ideal state, the polis makes privileges and rights available to all; however, they must be distributed according to individual contributions to the welfare of the community.

Aristotle (1891) believes that ruling and being ruled are natural social phenomena, and that among rational individuals ruling should be the province of those who are superior in reason. Since a priori reasoning cannot be employed to rank individuals in such a manner that their various potentialities are evidenced, the polis must offer an equitable alternative method, which Aristotle claims is found in the formulation of distributive justice. In this manner, Aristotle tries to fuse the value of a hierarchical structure with the value of equality. Thus, the value of justice orders all public actions with others to the common good, without making any unreasonable exceptions or giving anyone any unwarranted advantages.

Aristotle (1891) views justice from two vantage points: First, there is a broad sense of justice or general justice. Second, there is a narrow sense or particular justice. General justice, which he often calls legal or social justice, functions to direct action toward the common good - the welfare of society at large. That justice is a wider notion than law may be illustrated in Aristotle's delineation of particular justice.

Particular justice focuses on the partial or specific institutions within the general framework of society and these may be even further sub-divided. Particular justice is concerned with the differing types of interactions among private individuals, whose relationship to the social structure is comparable to that of the parts to a whole. For example, particular justice may be subdivided into (1) domestic justice, which governs the relations between outside workers in a household and the members of a household; (2) despotic justice, which refers to the relations between parent and child; (3) conjugal justice, which pertains to the relations between husband and wife. These distinctions suggest that there are aspects of justice where questions of law and formal social organization may not be directly applicable.

Although Aristotle usually considers justice from a particular point of view, he admits to the popular usage of general justice. Aristotle's treatment is especially noteworthy in the way in which he captures the antitheses and tensions of justice. Sociologically, his distinction between the two modes of justice is important because it tries to cover every area of human interaction. Justice is first an inherent part of group formation because it is a cohesive factor. On another level justice is external to the life of the group, it is justice which operates between individuals, families, and groups.' In this way, Aristotle attempts to overcome or limit the assertion of value-relativism. His theory of justice subsequently provides a criticism of the inflexibility of "legal justice" and its general inability to deal with the special circumstances of a concrete case. He insists on a judicious particularism in the application of law and the administration of justice.

Aristotle makes a number of important contributions to the Public Interest construct of justice. Many of his ideas are adopted and developed by other writers. For instance, most writers who work within a Public Interest framework would agree with Aristotle that the idea of justice extends beyond the mere legal (general) sense (See Sidgwick, 1962). It may be agreed that the legal sense of justice is perhaps the first and most commonly known formulation of justice. But this admission does not serve to detract from the Public Interest conception of justice, since the main point of departure is that justice extends beyond the limit of the law and the social order, and can even provide a basis for evaluating it.

Aristotle assumes that social organization and a consciousness of justice must presuppose any system of government. This suggests a natural justice. Proponents of a Public Interest version of justice would probably support the idea of natural justice in the sense intended by Aristotle. Hume (1955), for example, implies support for natural justice when he writes that "the state of society without government" is not only conceivable, but it is also "one of the most natural states of men" (501). Furthermore, he insists that justice is a prerequisite for the natural order; justice functions as the cohesive factor in the natural state (1894: 196-197). Accordingly, justice may even supply the basis for determining the goodness of positive law. Hume goes on to say, that when laws become "so perverse as to cross all interest of society" then the laws must forfeit their authority and "men judge by ideas of natural justice" (196-197).

Hume reasons that since a consciousness of justice underlies the well-being of society, it may be expressed in conventional terms. He argues that while individuals may disagree over certain details of the working out of justice, ultimately people's notions of justice correspond to one another. Justice rises out of the needs which are common to all within society. Here, Hume supposes that the question of justice is raised by scarcity. He makes the following observation:

> If nature supplied abundantly all our wants and desires . . . the jealousy of interest which justice supposes could no longer have a place (Rescher, 1966:107).

Hume (1955), concerning himself mainly with coherence of the utilitarian model, is content to enlist justice in its service by submitting that "public utility is the sole origin of justice" (43). For Hume, rules and laws and the social order are subsequently bound by convention and custom, and are justified by their public "utility". He suggests that in order to consider something, in the sense of the well-being of society, there must be a judgment of utility by a preponderance of individuals (Holt, 1970: 62). In this way, Hume (1955) develops a theory of justice in terms of a preponderance theory. This preponderance rests on the values which constitute personal interest and which engage the evaluative component in justice. He writes:

38

The original motive to the establishment of justice and sympathy with the public interest is the source of the normal approbation which attends the virtue (499-500).

His theory suggests that the concept of justice does not bring about immediate consensus or pleasure, since it depends on the circumstances which give rise to it. Hence, Hume (1961) writes that justice causes -

pleasure and approbation by means of an artifice or contrivance, which arises from the circumstances and necessity of mankind (430).

Accordingly, the implication is that justice is a commendatory concept which serves as an indicator of the degree to which social needs are met.

John Stuart Mill (1957) agrees with Hume that the sentimental aspect of justice is derived from utility. Mill, however, goes further and traces the obligatory element in justice to the concept of utility as well. But once he succeeds in connecting justice to utilitarianism, Mill seeks to prove that justice constitutes a limited class of phenomena of the socially "useful" (52). Mill writes that:

Justice is a name for certain classes of moral rules which concern the essentials of human well-being more nearly, and are therefore of more absolute obligation, than any other rules for guidance of life; and the notion which we have found to be of the essence of the idea of justice - that of a right residing in an individual - implies and testifies to this more binding obligation (73).

According to Mill, obligation is established to the extent that an individual's action or decision promotes the greatest general good, irrespective of how the greatest good is defined. Justice is based on the comparison of outcomes of other possible alternative actions assuming similar circumstances. When the selected actions or decisions result in less well-being when compared to another alternative, the decision or action is unjust or immoral.

The difference between justice and morality is ultimately that the consequences of justice are judged collectively and not individually. Mill suggests that obligation in justice "regarded collectively, stands higher on the scale of social utility, and is therefore of more paramount obligation than any other" (79). The collective is of particular significance, since it is believed the collective "concerns the essentials of human well-being, more nearly." Indeed, the well-being of the collective over the individual is "of more absolute obligation than any other rules of guidance of life" (73). While obligation, in this sense, is distinctly dependent on the collective conscious, the decision to act is still a private matter and rests on the individual's ability to comprehend the social good.

Using the principle of "good for good", Mill announces that "social utility is evident"; because when one rejects this principle of reciprocity, society is hurt. Mill expresses this in the following:

> He who accepts benefits and denies a return of them needed, inflicts a real hurt by disappointing one of the most natural and reasonable of expectations and one which he must at least tacitly have encouraged, otherwise the benefits would seldom have been conferred (75).

But justice, considered solely in terms of reciprocity, may just as easily turn into exchanging evil for evil, rather than good for good. Mill deals with this problem by providing a reconciliation of retaliative justice with the untilitarian philosophy. Mill does not treat this problem on the individual level, however, but, on the societal level. Mill begins by accepting the natural impulse to retaliate as a sentiment of justice but only in reference to those instances where the injury is to society at large, and only in those cases where their retaliative justice has a precise useful reformative function. By holding on to an intransigent individualism, and by identifying justice with the maximization of rights and social utility, Mill produces a concept of justice which is irreconcilable with anything but formal egalitarianism (376). In Mill's system equitable treatment is only a part of the concept of justice. The idea of equality has an instrumental function and is "a necessary condition of the fulfillment of other obligations of justice" (761). His notion of equality, however, is a distributive equality. He submits:

> If it is duty to do to each according to his deserts, returning good for good, as well as repressing evil by evil, ... it necessarily follows that we should treat all equally well (when no higher duty forbids) who have deserved equally well of us, and that society should treat all equally well who have deserved equally well of it, that is, who have deserved equally well absolutely.... But this great moral duty rests upon a still deeper foundation, being a direct emanation from the first principle of morals, and not a mere logical corollary from secondary or derivative doctrines. It is involved in

40

the very meaning of utility, or the greatest happiness principle. That principle is a mere form of words without rational signification unless one person's happiness, supposed equal in degree (with the proper allowance made for kind), is counted for exactly as much as another's. Those conditions being supplied, Bentham's dictum, 'everybody to count for one, nobody for more than one,' might be written under the principle of utility as a explanatory commentary (76).

This being the case, the justice or injustice of inequality is similarly to be decided only in terms of social utility. To this end, Mill proclaims: "justice has . . . two sides to it, which it is impossible to bring into harmony . . . social utility alone can decide the preference" (72).

By connecting justice with the principle of utility, the underlying assumption is that the value of the consequences is invariable and the same for everybody. In addition, this combination also implies the presumption of some sort of mathematical equation to come into play which suggests that certain consequences may be evaluated in terms of the magnitude of public interest or well being.

This, to be sure, creates distinct problems for a utilitarian model of justice. It provides the major critique of the perspective and therefore, is especially noteworthy from a developmental point of view. For example, Rawls (1958) rejects the idea that justice answers most fully to common interest or need. Furthermore, Rawls demands that justice is not merely a consequence, but that it must also supply the premise for any numerical calculation. He claims that Mill's brand of utilitarian justice will even accept slavery in the event that the advantages to the slave-holder or to the economy surpass the disadvantages to the slave. The proposition that justice must express the greater general satisfaction, rather than concern itself with the merits of each individual case denies the possibility of a "particular" justice within the framework of "general" justice. Rawls reasons that despite the possibility that a formula for justice gives general satisfaction, if it hampers even a tiny minority of an adequate life, justice is not obtained. First, Rawls believes that the more interests one has satisfied, the less one values the satisfaction. Second, he raises the issue that if justice results in treating equals equally and unequals according to their respective inequalities, the criteria of relevance must be considered. Rawls brings us back to Aristotle's original position.

Despite Rawl's rejection of Mill's justice as "fair dealing" based on the idea of reciprocity, his solution rests on the mutual realization in society that the "rational egoists" understanding that their competing interests can coexist as long as no-one is allowed to force his/her will against the rest (1958:164-194). Rawl's view of justice gives way to a body of regulations rising from the mutual recognition that they serve personal interests as well as social interest, given that others on whose acquiesence the individual depends, have interests that conflict with personal freedom. Justice, in this regulatory sense, can only work in the event that even when an individual's interests are discriminated against on some given occasion, the person can transcend personal need and still be able to appreciate the existence of the regulatory system underlying the concept of justice.

In this fashion, Rawls (1971) provides an added dimension to the conceptualization of justice. In his "justice as fairness", social cooperation is essential; it necessitates choosing together "in one joint act, the principles which are to assign basic rights and duties and to determine the division of social benefits" (9). Individuals, collectively, must determine in advance the way to regulate conflicting interests, and the constitutive elements of the foundation charter. Rawls further claims that the method underlying the judgment of "good" will serve to distinguish what is just. Thus, the process of justification involves a method of deliberation and judicious particularism. People's collective consciousness will govern the selection of principles and will determine the rationale to be adopted in the a specific contractual relation. Beyond this, Rawls suggests that a minimum constant adjustment is necessary so that the principles deduced from the choices do not conflict with the society's unshakable "common sense" convictions of right and wrong.

The implication of all of this is that justice may be sufficiently understood in terms of periodic program supplanting certain social values as they are summoned. Even if a particular program is comprehensive, it must be flexible enough to accommodate a myriad of alternatives. Justice, then, is inclined to be a concilatory concept.

Proudhon (1896) also proposes the unifying function of the concept of justice. But he does not rely on Utilitarianism to provide the rationale for his theory. Proudhon like Rawls attempts to effect a conciliation between the individual and society through a concept of justice. But, rather than attempting to blend the particular and general aspects of justice, Proudhon proceeds by integrating individuals in a transpersonal, anti-hierarchical order and making justice transcend its particular and general qualities. This is effected by relying on an "other-consciousness" which automatically effects respect for the individual, insofar as an individual is an indispensable member of a society and not merely the summation of its parts. For Proudhon, justice is only possible in a society which is economically characterized by "mutualism". Mutualism consists of every industry functioning by the voluntary association of producers, both industrial and agrarian, bound together by free contracts. Providing a regulating council, which represents the federation of economic associations, would be the state's primary function. Free credit and the creation of a People's Bank would cause an economic revolution and cause the disintegration of capitalism, and also cause the institution of justice based on mutualism.

Robert Hoffman's (1972) writings on Proudhon's concept of justice in his Revolutionary Justice describes it as follows:

> Proudhon's is an ideal of unity by means of the voluntary, rational recognition of the justice and the personal advantages of solidarity based upon the mutual recognition of rights and interests in all social relations with arrangements for reciprocal benefits" (227-259).

We may note that Rawls conception closely resembles Proudhon's in this particular sense. Both notions of justice are conciliatory and function as agents of social solidarity, working in the midst of diversity. Using the notion of mutual respect for individual differences, Proudhon and Rawls attempt to associate justice with reciprocal exchange and mutual benefit serving as its basis. The main difference between the two theories is that Proudhon arrives at his conclusions through a critique of capitalism and, thus, focuses on the economic aspects; while Rawls gets there via an intensive critique of utilitarianism and emphasizes the political variables.

In summary, justice from the Public Interest perspective is only achievable through acting for the common good. The degree to which a policy of justice disregards the various competing interests is to that extent injust. According to the Public Interest construct, justice is what individuals presumably want to achieve in part by associating together; and it is the condition for their associating that determines what must be done and what sort of regulations should be imposed upon individuals to maintain the relative harmony in society. The criterion is not inherently ethical because the concern is primarily given to actions which express the ideal of general welfare. This involves an emphasis of "other consciousness" and practicality. This perspective does not rely on any legal criterion since it does not emphasize the values of sactioned duty and stability. The proponents of this perspective are more interested in reformation than stability. Justice is a reforming agent rather than a stabilizing agent. What is unique about this view of justice is that it reflects the values of the cultural and institutional contexts within which it is considered. The diversity principle and the notion of judicious particularism are central to this perspective.

But there are also anti-utopian considerations, rising out of the major criticism which is generally leveled against this species of justice definitions. For example, it is often feared that individual needs or opinions would not be tolerated because they might undermine cohesion or the common goals of society. Taken to the extreme, this suggests that a Public Interest type justice would probably unload its affection onto some abstract notion of social good or to a statistical average (if such can be reasonably worked out). It is feared that given this basic orientation, fundamental policy in the name of the people will be sacrosanct, even in spite of the exposition of bureaucratic blunders. The corresponding paranoia which may evolve to reinforce this is that if ordinary men and women are encouraged to think for themselves they will soon think only of themselves. But most popular among the criticisms against a Public Interest version of justice is that it inevitably may point to an opportunistic type of justice. This criticism raises the spectre of traditional objections against justice, which a fundamentally Public Interest orientation finds difficult to resolve.

C. Individual Autonomy

> If I turn the inquiry to why nature brought forth man and why she set him above the other animals, would you then judge me to have left our topic, the question of justice, far behind?
> (Friedrich & Chapman, 1963: 127-128)

The Individual Autonomy construct of justice is predicated on the belief that the human being is in possession of some special qualities, and that the essense of being human must form the fundamental criterion for all valuation. Anything external to the nature of the human being cannot serve as a standard for establishing the hierarchy of values. The fact that individuals demonstrate the ability to raise questions over values and certain ideals in society indicates that the specialness of human nature defies any classification of the individual as a mere constitutive element in society. The search for a standard begins and ends with the human being or human dignity.

44

The Individual Autonomy construct is perhaps the most complex. It is the most prevalent and there are many variations to this basic theme. Among some of the individuals who may be associated with this general perspective are: St. Thomas Aquinas (1941-1945), Franz Brentano (1902; 1973), Cicero (1884), Giorgio Del Vecchio (1956), Thomas Hill Green (1901), Hugo Grotius (1925), Immanuel Kant (1884; 1959), Gottfried W. Leibniz (1956), John Locke (1958, 1948), Jacques Maritain (1951), Karl Marx (1959, 1962), Plato (1892), Adam Smith (1937), W. T. Stace (1937), Lawrence Stapleton (1944), Julius Stone (1965, 1966), to name a few.

A concept of justice based on social good or utility, and social order or positive law, is considered narrow by the proponents of the Individual Autonomy perspective. Any standard based on anything other than "human nature" is limited. First, individuals cannot be controlled totally; any government through its legal system pertains only to a small portion of human interactions, so any definitions which are legalistic cannot be applied generally. Second, the common good cannot transcend the individual good. The last test is justice for each and every individual human being. While other definitions are not entirely discarded, the contention is that justice based on human nature is the first and most fundamental formulation. The priority of human nature over social good and normative order in the concept of justice may be demonstrated in the following statement:

> Justice has its beginning in nature; then certain things become customary by reason of their utility; still later, both those that came from nature and those approved by custom were sanctioned by the fear of the law and religion (Cicero, 1884: 60).

The formulation of justice, which depends on human nature for its criterion suggests a myriad of questions which are treated in various degrees in the literature. The questions revolve around such issues as: volitional directedness, the scope of motivation, the ability to complete cognition, and the conscious appropriation and the transformation of self consciousness to human consciousness.

What is especially crucial to this general position is the assumption that what characterizes the individual also characterizes society. The belief is that when individuals realize their social essences and social interdependence, they will also realize their essential rights, their equal human status and their inner need to be fulfilled in the full sense of what it means to be a human being.

The most famous and perhaps most influential formulation in the entire history of the concept of justice, is the one the Roman legal philosophers enshrined in the Justinian Code: "Justice is the constant and perpetual will of rendering to each his right." The definition is even older than the Code. It is contained in the work of Cicero (1884) which has been translated as "giving to each his own." Jesus' advice to "Render unto Caesar that which is Caesars' and unto God that which is God's" is a direct parallel. This basic theme also appears in Plato's Republic: the last part is replaced with "what is due." Not much consideration has been given to the meaning of the concept of "due" as such; more commonly it is treated in the analysis of natural law or human rights.

Traditionally, justice, in the sense of the Individual Autonomy construct, is discussed with reference to natural law theories. The problematic of natural law points to the derivation of the natural order and to the determination of the nature of the individual, the hierarchical order of values based on the natural order. The basic assumption is that there is a natural hierarchy of values which underlie natural law; and, consequently, this also gives rise to the conception of justice. The emphasis here is on the constant features of human personality and social life as indicators of the natural order. The question is, however, whether the conception of justice presupposes the voluntary action of humankind or whether it is itself determined by individual volition? The answer to this question constitutes the basic approach to the treatment of justice from the perspective of Individual Autonomy.

For Plato justice is a reflection of the immutable hierarchical order of values. The only way Plato can approach the connotative meaning of justice is to reconstruct the hierarchical order of values which characterize human existence. In the Republic Socrates and the Sophist, Thrasymachus, are discussing the central question of the whole dialogue: What is Justice? Thrasymachus insists that justice simply means "in the interest of the stronger" (Plato, 1892: 338c–339c). Socrates, however, rejects Thrasymachus' formulation, arguing that it cannot be held synonymous with the concept of justice. Socrates suggests that many conceptions of justice are not definitions of justice but represent what in present terms may be described as sociological or psychological observations about the things which people label justice. But if Thrasymachus' definition represents a legitimate sociological observation which implies the use of the concept of justice – there is still the question of how the knowledge of justice is derived?

By attempting to derive a definition through a construction of an ideal state, Socrates tries to differentiate between the natural and the conventional meanings of justice.

46

He emphasizes the former. His distinction between the natural and the conventional is not derived from an analysis of a pre-social individual versus the socialized individual, but rather from the socially perfected individual, versus the socially debased. Moreover, the assumption appears to be that the perfection of the individual can only be discovered in the context of a perfect or just human society. This is perhaps a clue as to the nature of Socrates' and Thrasymachus' argument: The latter is concerned with the way things are usually evaluated. The former with what ought to be indicated by the ideal.

Socrates finally arrives at several formulations of justice which may be summarized by the following phrase: "Justice is everyone having and doing what is appropriate to him" (Plato, 1892: 483a, 434c). Accordingly, justice requires that everyone be assigned a function or such a job as he/she can perform well. But everyone does best that for which they are best fitted by nature. Justice exists, then, only in a society in which everyone does what he/she can do well, and in which everyone has what he/she can use well. Justice is identical with membership in such a society and devotion to such a society – a society according to nature. His insistence that justice results from each element in society doing the "appropriate" task, doing it well, and doing it consistently, has led to a great deal of criticism of Plato's system. Plato's recent critics who condemn the Republic's hierarchic structure as undemocratic, say little about its anticipation of modern phenomenological approach to the derivation of our knowledge of values or sociological systems that base social solidarity on a deliberate separation of social functions.

Through the middle ages, Christian thinking concerning the relationship between natural law and justice appeared to follow Plato's line of reasoning (Lodge, 1926). For Aquinas natural law rests on eternal law and divine rule and reason. The major rule is to behave according to reason (Aquinas, 1941-1945). The knowledge and implementation of natural law depends entirely on the degree to which rationality guides behavior in the individual in the direction for which humankind is preordained. This amounts to the notion that all individuals through reason have equal access to the ideal law of nature. The universal law of nature is made accessible by treating human law as an expression of natural law, which is itself an expression of the Supreme Being's rational will guiding the universe.

Grotius (1625), in the late Middle Ages, provides the antithesis to Aquinas' idealist explanation. He claims that the cognition of justice and the natural order may exist even if God does not. Grotius argues that an individual is bound by the law of nature, even if one supposes that there is no Supreme Being, because natural law derives from two human qualities of sociability and rationality. The essential human dependence upon society dictates the minimum conditions of social harmony. In this regard, natural law is a universal test of the application of positive law. Justice is now no longer grounded on theology, but is developed on the basis solely of a natural hierarchy of values imminent in the world; and primarily on the foundation, once again, of human nature (Strauss, 1953: 129).

Individuals, by nature social beings, are so constituted that they cannot live or live well, except by living together: "humanity itself is sociality" (129). In every human action, reference is made to interdependence. Sociality does not progress from "a calculation of the pleasures" taken from expectations based on association, but arises from the "pleasure of association". Since the individual is first and foremost naturally social, the "perfection" of individual "nature includes the social virtue par-excellence, justice; justice and right are natural" (129).

Leibniz presents the most congruous elaboration of the perfectionistic position. Like the former philosophies, Leibniz (1956) affirms that social organization depends upon universal reason. He compares justice, which he considers is an immutable standard of reason, to the no less immutable characteristic of the eternal truths which serve as principles of geometry and arithmetic. This position precludes the tension between the individual and the universal or between the microcosm and the macrocosm. It allows the synthesis of the whole with the parts. By making every community and group the medium for the realization of justice, no privileges whatever are extended to the state.

Locke (1943), in contrast to Liebniz and the other theorists discussed above, suggests that justice and the idea of natural human right can only be understood by hypothetically studying an individual in a state of nature apart from society. This hypothetical abstraction leads him to the conclusion that "all men are naturally in . . . a state of perfect freedom to order their actions and dispose of their possessions and persons as they think fit" (227). This right to live, as one likes, is not conferred by society or government, but, naturally belongs to the human being. It is natural for individuals to desire autonomy and to respect it. He states that natural human right to be free "belongs to man as man and not as a member of society." He continues:

> The law of nature . . . which obliges everyone, and reason which is that law, teaches all mankind who will but consult it, that being all equal and

independent, no one ought to harm another in his life, health, liberty or possessions (6).

But the passage indicates that for Locke, no rule of law of nature is known innately. For him, perhaps, the only universal principle is the "desire of happiness, and an aversion of misery . . . " Thus, Locke maintains that happiness is an innate natural human right. But because there is no duty attached to this right, no natural law can be derived from this right. Therefore, the process of reasoning alone determines what individuals can know about the law of nature and what justice consists of. When conflict over rights arise, Locke argues that life presupposes happiness, hence, the desire for living comes before the desire for happiness and is decisive. Rationality dictates that an individual is "master of himself and his own life and has a right, too, to the means of preserving it" (Straus, 1953: 227). Furthermore, given that all individuals are equal in respect to the pursuit of happiness and of self-preservation it follows that all humans are equal in the last analysis, in spite of any inequalities in other respects. Consequently, Locke implies that justice is based on an absolute equality and the dictates of reason. Awareness of "mutual security" or "the peace and safety" of humankind are naturally deduced. However, the laws of nature are not complied with universally - not everyone follows the dictates of reason. So Locke considers a system of government which is based on reason and natural law: a government which protects an individual's inalienable rights.

As with philosophy in general, Kant's (1884) critique of knowledge constitutes a turning point for the theory of natural law and the notion of human right, and subsequently of the idea of justice. For Kant, there is natural right resting upon pure rational principles, a priori. Since natural human right is that "which is knowable purely a priori by everyone's reason," it underlies the constitution of a civil society (429b). It supplies a criterion for the positive law since it "provides the conditions of such a constitution"; and, therefore, is "not to be infringed upon by the statutory laws of such a constitution". The knowledge of natural human right or rational principles a priori, are expressed through a concept of justice. Justice as a subjective consciousness of the objective order (hierarchal order of values) is identical in all humankind. Kant's position represents a type of synthesis of the two approaches for natural law. The Kantian notion of justice is comprised of the synthesis of equality and liberty. When the normative order or the demands of the state contradict an individual's consciousness of justice (his/her natural will), the individual is no longer obligated to conform to the rules.

49

Granting this idea of justice, distinctly revolutionary and anarchic features are introduced. While it is admitted that the state can provide a guarantee of the normal coincidence between law and the individual consciousness of justice, it is held that when conflict develops, the state may be relinquished of its authority by the recourse to individual conscience, which is, in the end, decisive. In Kant's conceptualization, an unlimitable depth of subjectivism and individualism embraces the idea of justice.

His theory of individualism is key to the distinction between morality and justice. He submits that the social order, as contrasted with individual consciousness, is devoid of any real or direct system of valuation and is limited to the external relations among people. Justice, which is derived from an inner consciousness of the individual essence and social interdependence applies to the regulation of external activity; but to morality is delegated exclusively concern with the private life. Kant's (1959) celebrated definition of justice is as follows:

> Justice is the external liberty of each person, limited by the liberty of all others (49).

This theory is of special significance because it guards the essential rights of human beings. It protects individuality: it protects one's religious, political, esthetic leanings, and general opinions from all intervention by the state. This is accomplished by denoting clearly a line of demarcation between morality and justice, in such a manner that the latter may not serve as a pretext for such intervention. To this end, justice functions as an external check imposed upon divergent wills. In spite of Kant's emphasis on freedom, society still serves to restrict individual freedom. Kant's justice remains divorced from the empirical world. By making freedom part of consciousness and the internal realm and by keeping law and society confined to the external world of compulsion, Kant failed to integrate freedom in society or the experience of justice in society.

Del Vecchio presents an interesting variation and more contemporary treatment of Kant's fundamental principles. He writes:

> Justice, in this its supreme expression requires that every subject be recognized and treated by every other as absolute principle of his own acts ... Justice requires that in every social relation there should be presupposed as ideal basis an original "right to solitude" so that in the actual concrete structure of social life there may be re-affirmed and developed (it may be even through

apparent denials, as moments of a dialectic process) that ideal element of autonomy which constitutes the inviolable essence of the person (Baldwin, 1966: 7).

Both Kant (1959) and Del Vecchio (1956) contend that justice essentially rests on the maximization of autonomy of each human person living in association with others. This is how Del Vecchio puts it:

> Justice desires every subject to be recognized and treated by every other as an absolute principle of his own action. Justice desires that in reciprocal treatment the meta-empiric identity of nature should be taken into consideration, with the consequent exclusion of any disparity not founded on the effective manner of being and operation of each individual: for these purposes all behavior should be objectively referred to the same absolute standard (1956: 119-120).

The natural hierarchy of values suggests standards which obligate individuals and demands obedience. In a scientific sense, the formula expresses certain observed uniformities of events. There is a demand for a respect for individualism and autonomy within that order.

Reacting against the perverse individualism of capitalism of the industrial development, the early socialist doctrines of the nineteenth century (Saint Simon, Auguste Comte, and Karl Marx) exhibited attitudes of hostility to the prevailing ideas of justice and law. For example, there is no place for justice in the analyses of economic relations in Marx's and Engel's work. To them justice is a mere mirage produced by capitalistic preconceptions. They ridicule the concept and consider it a mask for capitalist exploitation and hypocrisy. "Life is not determined by consciousness, but consciousness of life" (Marx & Engels, 1947: 15). For Marx, justice represents the supreme expression of the "superstructure", and is the unconscious or semi-conscious ideological reflection of economic relations as evident in: "justice for the rich and not for the poor" (Berman, 1950: 22). (This may remind one of Thrasymachus' observations in the Republic that "justice is in the interest of the stronger.") In a capitalistic society justice can only be understood as "the ideal expression of the dominant material relationships" (Marx & Engels, 1947: 39). Marx and Engels write:

> The class which has the means of material production at its disposal, has control at the same time over the means of mental production, so that thereby, generally speaking, the ideas of those who

51

lack the means of mental production are subject to it (39).

The socialist rejection of justice is carried on in the following progression: The criticism first points to capitalist injustice pronounced in the inequalities or unfairness of distribution. The concept of justice is considered ludicrous since its function is to obscure the essential nature of exploitation. In the context of capitalism, justice is considered phenomenally impossible. The argument is that the attempts to rectify "injustices" on the distributive side necessarily lead to accepting the notion that equilibrium may be established in spite of the irreconcilable forces inherent in a capitalist society. Following, it is alleged that the proponents of the concept of justice misconstrue the nature of class conflict, and only serve to distract the proletariat from their responsibility to the future. The implication is that the concept of justice in the distributive sense is essentially misleading, if not dangerous.

However, this denunciation of justice does not render Marxism ethically devoid as is supposed by some critics. Justice apart from its "bourgeois" connotation is seminal to Marxism. Lindsay (1942) has said of Marx: "His fundamental passion is a passion for justice" (114). An interpreter of Marxism, E. H. Carr (1934), also has suggested that justice is the moral theme of Marx's principal work:

> Marx demonstrated . . . that the victory of the proletariat would be the victory not only of brute force, but of abstract justice (83).

It is Marx's sensitivity to the idea of the human right to a decent life in which individuals can share equally of worldly goods, that gives him the impetus to create the notion of communism, which for Marx is, the only system which permits the realization of justice. His rejection of bourgeois ideology and justice as false consciousness is a modern version of Thrasymachus' position or sociological observation of what people call justice. Correspondingly, in the Marxian system, the values, standards and rules of capitalism are only reflections of the cultural superstructure, which results from the socioeconomic base in society. On the other hand, in Marx's formulation of ideal communism, one is reminded of the Socratic notion of justice in which the individual returns to a natural ideal existence. Marx in his Economic and Philosophical Manuscripts writes:

> Communism is the positive abolition of private property of human self-alienation, and thus the real appropriation of human nature through and for man. It is, therefore, the return of man himself as

a social, i.e., really human being, a complete and conscious return which assimilate all the wealth of previous development. Communism as a fully developed naturalism is humanism and as a fully developed humanism is naturalism.... (Fromm, 1961: 127).

Marx is a man who is so disturbed by the injustices of capitalist society of his time, that he calls for a better day of freedom and justice. He proposes a program to implement the fulfillment and expression of certain natural values and ideals for human life. Marx insists that knowledge, action, ideas and the social system in which values are developed, including moral values and the economic basis of a society are inseparably intertwined. He attempts to study society in order to discover the dynamics which motivate individual behavior. He sees the necessity of active involvement by individuals (i.e., the interaction between mind and experience) if the world is to be made better. A theme running through his entire life is expressed in his Theses on Feuerbach: "The philosophers have only interpreted the world differently, the point is to change it." (Marx & Engels, 1947: 199) Even as Marx focuses on historic change he holds that there are also laws of change and invariant relations. The unique character of Marxism lies in the particular manner through which a systematic understanding of human nature is applied to the doctrine of historic movement.

Marxism means to go to "the root of things", which he insists is the individual in an "ensemble of social relations" (Dupre, 1966: 87-108). For Marx the true essence of human nature appears only when society and the individual exist in the state of union with nature.

Thus society is the consummated oneness in substance of man and nature - the true resurrection of nature - the naturalism of man and the humanism of nature both brought to fulfillment (Dupre, 1966:133).

The individual is basic to Marx's philosophy. The conception of the individual is not based on some ideal abstraction, the universality of human beings depends on the existence of concrete individuals, i.e., human beings exist empirically. But what separates his version of individualism from what he calls the abstract - metaphysical concept of the individual, is his insistence that the real essence of the individual can only evolve from social relations. He demands, however, that the social category does not make the individual subordinate to it. Rather he suggests that we should not set 'Society' up against as an abstraction opposed to the individual (Marx & Engels, 1947).

The ultimate goal of socialism is justice granting individual freedom or as Marx put it: "the association of free individuals."

> Only in community with others has each individual the means of cultivating his gifts in all directions; only in the community, therefore is personal freedom possible .... In the real community the individuals obtain their freedom in and through their association (Marx & Engels, 1947: 74-75).

Marx's humanism is at the root of his criticism of capitalistic justice. He opposes capitalism because it prevents the union of individuals and nature, and prevents the universal expression of human beings as free individual beings. Marx's (1956) central argument against capitalism is that it prevents the union of the individual and society. The indignation of the proletariat stems from the fact that capitalism contradicts human nature. It transforms the "person individual" into a "class individual" (Fromm, 1961). Class societies, accoring to Marx, set a premium on a dehumanized egotistical materialism.

The emergence of "the truly human" or "true individuality" is not just an abstract idea by is conditioned by the classless society which Marx defined as the "real appropriation of human essence through and for man."

> Ideas never lead beyond the established situation, they only lead beyond the ideas of the established situation. In fact, ideas cannot realize anything. The realization of ideas requires men who apply a practical force" (Marx & Engels, quoted in Dupre, 1966:140).

Marx's criticism of class orders is not confined to economic and political structures alone, but it moves into the moral sphere.

The elimination of the antithesis: individual versus society, provides the moral basis for Marxian ethics. However, a philosophy which makes the historic flux supreme without relating it to some standards which are not in flux suggests a relativistic perspective. Questions of "right" and "good" and "justice" sometimes turn into questions of "right" and "good" and "justice" for whom?

Hence, Marxism is often reproached for having a partisan conception of justice, upholding the interests of the proletariat as against those of other groups. His doctrine of the class struggle is condemned as generating or at least fostering social conflict. In answer to these charges, Lenin (1927-1942) points out that the idea of class struggle "was not created by Marx, but by the bourgeois before Marx," and that, therefore, it was "simply untrue that the main point in the teaching of Marx is the class struggle." Lenin maintains that far from welcoming it, Marxism aims to eliminate class conflict. Lenin suggests that this point, focal to Marxian thought, is clarified by reference to the category of alienation which Marx borrows from Hegel.

Marx's use of the term "alienation" is not confined to only the social or economic areas. The Marxist concept of alienation is the secular equivalent of sin, since alienation suggests that humankind is not what it ought to be (Marx, 1959: 8). Marx employs it in his economic analyses with definite implications for ethics and even for an idea of justice. He expresses this by pointing to the injustice of the depersonalizing consequences of capitalist production. Marx's complaint is that under capitalism the individual produces only to have; and moreover, to have for him/herself, thereby violating the universal human function (Fromm, 1961: 46-48). Marx raises the question of utility or of how the economic process satisfies human needs. It is a question of ultimate directives. And the Marxian aim is to abolish the very conditions which make the use of harsh means necessary. The final goal is the classless or "human" society. Karl Popper (1963) in his book, The Open Society and Its Enemies, summarizes the significance of Marx in the following statement:

> . . . his criticism of capitalism was effective mainly as a moral criticism. Marx shows that a social system can as such be unjust; that if the system is bad, then all the righteousness of the individuals who profit from it is a mere sham righteousness, is mere hypocrisy. For our responsibility extends to the system, to the institutions which we allow to persist (211).

Marx (1959) defends his focus on the working class as the bearer of true social justice by noting its distinction from other historical classes. While the bourgeois is concerned with establishing its own mastery, the proletariat is laboring to abolish not only the capitalist order but also "its own supremacy as a class." It cannot emancipate itself without "at the same time, and once and for all emancipating society at large from all exploitation, oppression, class distinction and class struggles" (8).

The value of individual autonomy generally, permits an important conclusion to be drawn - namely, that norms or laws which do not recognize and respect an individual as such, but instead degrade that individual to the status of a mere object, are not binding, even when they are obligatorily carried out. Kant not only expressed this conclusion but he made it the very center of his ethics. And it is exactly this logic that Marx employs, when he predicts the destruction of capitalism.

Not only is the society which demeans the individual doomed to lose its approbative base, the individual is obligated to change it. The general assertion is that an individual respects individual autonomy because a right by virtue of being a right obliges others to respect it. Justice, in the sense of Individual Autonomy, is considered to be naturally obligatory independent of the concept of positive law and utility or social good. For Marx, the idea of natural duty to behave justly is derived from the social nature of the individual which is given full expression only in a classless society. Kant's idea of obligation is expressed in terms of categorical imperatives, i.e., one must ascribe to what is just because it is one's personal duty to do so as a human being. Following, justice includes a distinct inner moral obligatory element which is distinct from the punitive and teleological right suggested by the other constructs of justice.

The Individual Autonomy construct of justice does not focus on the consequences of actions nor on the extent to which actions are practical for the attainment of certain goals of society. It does not rely on the might of the state, a regulatory system or social pressure. Rather, it emphasizes an inner consciousness of immediate actions of individuals with respect to other individuals. Justice is not limited by a consciousness of formal patterns of behavior. It embraces the whole range of knowledge about human interaction. This framework involves the generally summarized experience of individual's social life in the way in which persons become conscious of and realize their essence and subsequently, their interest for self-control in society.

Justice, in the sense of the Individual Autonomy construct, seems to derive from the idea that with the acquisition of knowledge (science) and with the perfection of the human personality, the phenomenon of justice in society will become an increasing reality. The general feeling is that essentially there is a common hierarchy of values, but this is obscured by individual symbolic expression and interpretation and culture. Assuming that the individual is basically rational and good, and given the freedom to express one's humanity, the individual will progress toward a rational and just social existence.

There are many varying philosophies which have attempted to prove the manner in which human nature can be known. What is significant in the various arguments about justice is that there is a basic agreement that some order of values exists. Consequently, the admission that some order of values exist suggests that justice flows from nature, and is not dependent on the positive law or the social good.

On the anti-utopian side, the critique of the Individual Autonomy formulation of justice suggests that the mere advocation of such values as "liberty", "human right", "self-determination", and "integration" does not in and of itself guarantee the attainment or realization of them; nor does it make individuals any more humane. And it is not all that clear that everyone desires total freedom; there are those who would forfeit some freedom for security and certainty.

D. Summary

A review and content analysis of the literature on justice suggests that there are at least three fundamental sets of values, which are typically associated with the concept of justice. The constructs of justice demonstrate fundamentally different sets of attitudes and assumptions about human nature and society. It is assumed that these three basic sets of criteria are exhaustive at their level of interpretation. Moreover, each construct represents a distinct master principle. For example, a situation may be assessed as "just" on principle according to the importance of value of the (A) social order (Normative Conformity); (B) social well-being (Public Interest); or (C) individual freedom (Individual Autonomy).

Irrespective of the specific context in which justice is considered, its conceptual significance is tied to the pronouncement of certain values in culture, which guide individuals in association with one another. Since justice functions to guide social interaction, it ultimately provides a criterion for evaluating the interaction. Justice, therefore, is a distinctly motivational concept. As such, it implies certain directives by which action may be predicted. The criteria elements of justice (ideation, evaluation, and prescription) provide the framework which is used for the content analysis of different theories of justice, and for the development of the three constructs of justice.

The Normative Conformity construct of justice attempts to capture an idea of justice which depends on a normative system of organization which incorporates a system to enforce the order and assure stability or continuity over time. This theme is traditionally enclosed in discussions of positive law. When the issue of justice is raised, the resolution in terms of the Normative Conformity construct includes the support for a social order, and the ability to objectively determine the appropriate behavior in reference to that order. If the results of the behavior or action maintains the social order or is consistent with it, the action is to that extent judged to be just.

A Public Interest construction of justice usually subsumes theories which consider the maximization of rights or interests in a pluralistic society. This type of reflection ultimately pays close attention to the degree of social solidarity, with justice functioning as the moving or cohesive force. Assuming the conflict of interests, the purpose of justice is to maximize their expression or assume their co-existence. Mild regulations are only indicated when the social conscience needs articulation. Justice, in the sense of a collective social solidarity, is primarily a conflict resolving agent, which is constantly moving toward the social well-being. Accordingly, it distinctly focuses on the special circumstances constituting the conflict, and seeks to obtain an equitable solution for all interests involved. This construct has its roots in utilitarian philosophy, and in some socialistic philosophy, and particularly in theories of distribution.

The Individual Autonomy construct of justice centers around the values of individuals, personal freedom, dignity and integrity in social life. Historically, natural law, rationality, volition and the individual capacity for moral judgment are among the contributory themes of this construct. This conception of justice is generally believed to rise forth from a mutual respect for human dignity and freedom of expression. Values are to be judged and ranked as greater or lesser contributions to self-realization. Justice, which is for some the highest value, is the greatest expression or fulfillment of the personality. Freedom of action or expression is supported to the extent that it contributes to the self-realization of an individual without interfering with the self-realization of others. The concern, then, turns specifically to an inner consciousness of right and wrong and social interdependence. This pertains to the ability of individuals to respect each other through an inner consciousness of human dignity, and the need for liberty.

The reference to individual is not just in the singular sense, as in the relationship of one person to another; individual may also refer to an aggregate body (group, corporation, country, etc.). Following, any individual entity may demand a justice giving it due regard and right to autonomy. In the Individual Autonomy construct of justice the focus is on the individual as a distinct entity of a greater whole which derives the right to be creative within the greater whole.

Generally, the Individual Autonomy construction of justice suggests that the individual is internally answerable for a discharge of duty; and relys on the conviction that justice is approached by the contribution that it, as a value, makes to the harmonious perfection of the human capacity to move toward the full realization and expression of human nature.

Since any one theory of justice can reflect individual bias or logical error, the constructs of justice have been developed to help overcome these problems and to clarify the phenomenological nature of justice. The constructs of justice must be considered more reliable as indicators of the rudimentary social phenomena or values which comprise the social knowledge of justice in society, if, for no other reason, than because individual logical inconsistencies and mistakes may be neutralized over time or in common attitudes.

There are several assumptions underlying the present conceptualization. First, it is assumed that a writer's definition of justice represents an interpretation of some portion of reality. Furthermore, the confirmation or repetition of any particular interpretation by other writers in other time frames suggests a certain degree of validity of its phenomenal existence.

History may provide proof that the variety of formulations of justice proposed here do exist in culture. The literature on justice may be taken as a reflection of the cultural expression of justice. The three types of definitions can be identified in varying degrees in the literature. (For a brief summary of all three constructs see Table 1.) Which theme is prevalent at any one time in history often seems to depend on the precise historical epoc or context in which the question of justice emerges. Perhaps, the interplay between the utopian or anti-utopian characteristics associated with each construct influence the level of awareness of social problems in society and forms the critique which gives rise to innovation or change in culture with respect to justice concepts.

What complicates the whole process is that the celebration of humanity through the joining together of the healing expression of the general welfare, and the growing acceptance of human nature, and the value of litigation in society are all valued yet the different value sets contradict one another. This may create major confrontations with the existing institutions and structures in society. The possibility of all three mutually exclusive formulations of justice must necessarily challenge certain existing institutions and distinctly complicate the realization of a unified conceptualization of justice.

TABLE ONE

SUMMARY OF THE HISTORICAL CONSTRUCTS OF JUSTICE

Constructs of Justice	Recurrent Theme	Primary Associative Values	Major Historical Context for Development of Theme	Related Concepts or Vocabulary	Main Criticism (Anti-utopic Features)
NORMATIVE CONFORMITY	Social Order; Traditional Continuity	Stability; Santioned Duty	Positive Law	Conformity "Law and Order" Legal Objectivity Legal Realism	Oppression; Loss of Relevance
PUBLIC INTEREST	Maximization of Rights and Interests; Social Good	Proportionate Equality; Judicious Particularism	Utilitarianism Socialism	Common Good; Collective Welfare; Co-operation; Community Consciousness Compromise; Collective Pragmatism	Anti-individualism (Where individual Lost and Becomes a Mere Cog or Insignificant Entity in Society)
INDIVIDUAL AUTONOMY	Individual Freedom; Human Dignity	Human Perfectionism; Inner Consciousness	Natural Law Philosophy	Liberty; Self-Determination Integration; Moral Responsibility	Lack of Social Responsibility; Exploitation of the weak.

60

Chapter Four

THE CONCEPTUAL DIMENSIONS OF JUSTICE

Two basic questions are endemic to the relationship between the theoretical constructs of justice and the portion of reality which is typically associated with each of them: What common elements usually constitute the goal of justice and its capacity to meet human needs? And, what are the variety of ways in which these elements may be expressed? With these questions in mind, the aim of this chapter is to specify with the help of the literature, the phenomenological content of justice, and to understand the conditions that subvert and sustain it.

Most authors concerned with justice would probably argue that, in spite of their own specific orientation, their respective theory has tapped the actual phenomenon of justice, and that their theory does and must resemble some aspect of reality. Each theory of justice found in the literature focuses on some social phenomena, and articulates certain sets of values which are deemed essential to the meaning of justice. For example, justice is often equated with such ideas as equality, fairness, impartiality, lawfulness, etc.

The assumptions and issues, which are at the core of the intellectual debate over the content of justice, are, perhaps, key to the phenomenal meaning of justice. The intellectual arguments are not only indicative of the distinction or emphasis of justice, but they demonstrate recurring associative ideas or values. The continuing debate in the literature over the nature of justice provides the basis for the development of the historically most prevalent associative ideas or conceptual dimensions of justice.

The determination of what conceptual dimensions are most important to the understanding of justice has been based on the following criteria: (1) most commonly discussed (popularity); (2) most emphasized (average number of pages devoted to topic); (3) application to all three constructs; and (4) intuitive relevance to the concept of justice. The issues associated with justice and their logical linkage to the constructs of justice have been developed from the following sources: First, the literature which yields a picture of the most "common problems" and most "emphasized problems"; second, the logical implications of the master principles underlying the historical constructs (for instance, the notion of individual leads to the notion of self-consciousness); third, the problems which seem to be associated with the master principles that are widely covered in the continuing debate over what is justice.

61

The major issues or philosophical dilemmas raised in the literature on justice must be stated, however, in such a manner that all three constructs of justice can be aligned with them for comparative purposes. This is best accomplished by logically patterning the constructs of justice according to selected pairs of mutually exclusive ideas, which meet the established criteria. Following, the most important issues debated in the literature on justice may be expressed in the form of a unique set of conceptual dimensions. The pairs of ideas comprising each conceptual dimension do not represent direct opposites in meaning, but they do represent contrasting ideas. Since the scheme has to assume a certain degree of generality, there may be a variety of terms and different shades of meaning associated with any general concept. Thus, the precise definition ascribed to the conceptual dimensions are not found in their exact form anywhere in the literature on justice. Nor is the exact combination of ideas found anywhere in the writing on justice. The approach represents a middle range level of generality. The purpose is to capture the overall picture of the major themes and theoretical dilemmas which accompany the literary characterization of justice. The following pairs of ideas are thus proposed to represent the major conceptual dimensions of justice: sameness/diversity; inter-personal subjectivity/-impersonal objectivity; improvement/ stability; other-conscious-ness/ inner-consciousness; perfectionism/practicality; and sanctioned duty/private duty. It is generally assumed that this list of conceptual dimensions comprises the ontological meaning of justice. The list is considered reasonably inclusive. It seeks to explain other dimensions or ideas found in the litera-ture; but, it, itself, cannot be explained by any other dimen-sions.

With the help of the literature and given the logic implied in the master principles, it will be seen that the constructs of justice exhibit different patterns of conceptual dimensions. The patterns show: (1) where the constructs of justice overlap with one another; (2) exactly on which points they differ with one another; and (3) precisely why they are unique. With the aid of the conceptual dimensions, the three historical constructs of justice suggest a method for the study of how the various notions of justice are espoused and predicted. For example, the dimensions which predominate in personal conceptions of justice or institutional expressions of justice may be used to determine which construct of justice is approximated. Moreover, the degree to which certain dimensions actually influence expectations or actions concerning justice, is the extent to which this conceptual scheme becomes instrumental in a predictive model of justice.

The underlying assumption here is that ideas have structure in culture. Our method suggests how such structures may be uncovered and studied. The conceptual scheme of justice may serve to discover the forms of phenomenal justice insofar as it expresses certain selected concrete values. These values, then, define the lines of justification which may be pursued both in future practice or in theory. The conceptual scheme of justice is intended to suggest not only a methodology for the investigation of the expression of justice in reality, but of the expression of other concepts as well. In this sense, the conceptual scheme introduced here may be a link between knowledge and society.

If only a portion of reality is absorbed by the human mind, then, given the nature of the conceptualization of justice, a certain part of that knowledge can be investigated. Because the conceptualization of justice may illuminate the genesis, and the substance of the relationship between reality and thought structures, it may serve as an analytical tool for a sociology of knowledge.

A. Sameness versus Diversity

Artistotle observed that "all men hold that justice is some kind of equality" (Bedau, 1967: 18). Perhaps one of the most common symbols for justice is represented by scales suggesting balance or equiparation. The importance of the controversy over the dimension of equality in the theories of justice cannot be avoided. Although the treatment of equality as a problem of justice has been represented in countless formulations and frequently confused, this cannot be used as an indictment of the validity of the phenomenal association of equity with justice. This is not to say, however, that the concept of justice can be reduced to notions of equality or resolved merely in such terms. Given the variety of types of egalitarian equations which have been proposed by the many writers of justice, the problem is how to present the underlying egalitarian principle which presuppose justice.

The question is ultimately whether one should emphasize the similarities or the differences among humankind when considering an equitable and just resolution. There is certainly ample evidence of the phenomenal inequalities among human beings (e.g., innate capacities, status, etc.); just as there are frequent experiences of the phenomenal equality in the sense of a fundamental identity of individuals with the species of humankind. The simultaneous apprehension of both the similarities and the differences among individuals possibly leads to the basic problem of the indeterminateness of the essential quality of human beings. Thus, Aristotle says that: "Injustice

63

arises when equals are treated unequally, and also when unequals are treated equally" (Ginsberg, 1965: 7).

For example, English Common Law is generally grounded on the idea that justice can only be accomplished by holding all individuals equal before the law. It seeks to eliminate special privileges based upon unwarranted or exaggerated emphasis on individual differences. Indeed, the class of beings who are ideally the object of the similarity principle consists of all of humankind. The reference to the element of universality suggests that the demand of justice is to extend the fundamental rights or benefits which are due to all groups or all types of individuals. Kelly (1956) writes: "Justice is the effort of man to repair the inequality of nature" (97).

In contrast, the Hindu believe that differences among individuals in society are central to their legal indentity. Accordingly, the village councils, employing the Hindu philosophy, seek to compromise the issues between the conflicting parties. The goal is to abate the conflict and to promote harmony. Justice is generally a function of differential treatment grounded upon any pre-existing inequalities. Difference of treatment, however, should match the differences of the situations in order for justice to be realized. In this sense, the standard is not based on an absolute but on a type of proportional notion of equality.

Even though both legal systems may be differentiated according to their points of emphasis, it is important to stress that the two approaches to equality are necessarily considered by both systems. Preference for either position suggests both elements of justice and injustice.

The relationship between the meaning of commutative justice and distributive justice may be relevant to this discussion. Commutative justice seeks the similarities of each and every juridical act, and attempts to insure equal handling. Justice, in this sense, consists of rendering to every individual the exact measure of his/her dues, without regard for any personal worth or merits. It places all individuals on a horizontal plane.

Distributive justice, however, relies on the notion of proportional equality which takes into account individual differences or capacities and efforts in resolving conflict or conferring benefits. It does not consider all individuals as equally deserving, or as equally blame-worthy. It discriminates between them, observing a just proportion and comparison. It places individuals on a vertical plane. Homan's (1961) definition is especially fitting:

64

By equality we do not mean the equality of all members of a group but equality within layers or strata - the rough equality with one another of members who are at the same time superior or inferior to others (362).

There may be two basic types of justifications considered in the distributive sense of justice: The first takes into account the variables of social position, or in Linton's (1936) terminology, "ascription". The second takes into account social action, or according to Linton's phraseology, "achievement". This set of ideas demonstrates the questions of dealing with individuals in accordance with their status or in accordance with what their actions may represent. Stated another way, one is either concerned with who an individual is and what a situation constitutes, or with what an individual is doing and what the situation signifies. The former stresses social roles as indicated by class, age, sex, professions, etc. The latter refers to observable behavior or social action, as for instance, the performance record of certain individuals. The problem which is encountered in acquiring a just resolution often lies in making the appropriate assessment. The position one occupies or the specific actions which are emphasized can be irrelevant to a given issue of justice.

For example, there is still a controversy over the justness of the 1974 grant of immunity to former President Nixon. Some argue that the immunity was granted irrespective of his alleged misdeeds, but on the basis of his former presidential status, which is considered by many to be irrelevant to the issue of justice. The supporters of the decision of immunity insist that the suffering which resulted from resigning the presidency was a punishment comparable to that of any citizen of a lower status who is punished by a court. Thus, part of the justification of the immunity decision was considered in a distributive or proportional sense; and it was presented on an ascriptive basis.

The Normative Conformity construct of justice and the Individual Autonomy construct of justice both tend to emphasize "sameness" in their respective formulations. The Public Interest construct of justice, however, is unique in stressing "diversity" in just resolutions.

The Normative Conformity construct of justice is built on the recurring premise that there is a general consensus over the formation of a normative social order or the state. It follows that there is an implied agreement over the existence of laws or the state for the purpose of protecting individuals in social life. Therefore, the protection of individuals implied from the guarantee of the normative order must be extended to every member of the society equally. We can infer from this that sameness of need and sameness of application are essential in a formulation of justice.

The logical meaning of justice based on the postulate of social order suggests, that, first, individual differences should be ignored for the sake of social order; and, second, that when conferring rights or imposing duty certain similarities should be held constant. Yet the Normative Conformity construct does not treat children as adults or the insane as sane. However, the positions supporting Normative Conformity justice indicate that to establish the relevance of justice, differences are considered to be beyond the domain of the principle of sameness. Accordingly, Kelsen (1957) writes:

> The principle of equality as a postulate directed at the authority creating the law meaning equality in the law, should not be confused with the principle of equality before the law, which is directed at the authorities applying the law to concrete cases. It means that law-applying organs shall not, in deciding a case, make a difference that is not provided for in the law to be applied, that is to say, they shall apply the law as it should be applied according to its own meaning (15).

The idea is that equality under the law as a criterion of justice is determined by the extent to which the commonalities are established. According to Perelman (1963) the test of the grounds for the justification of certain similarities among individuals usually depends on the worthiness of the argument to a "universal audience" of "reasonable men" (130-193). To this end, the function of justice is to establish a standard for equitable judgment, and to provide a phenomenal common basis for a legal identity among individuals.

The Individual Autonomy construct of justice also stresses the principle of sameness over diversity. Different philosophers or theorists, of course, have very different ways of expressing this dimension. For example, in Kant's justice, which illustrates his moral idealism, the idea of sameness is represented in terms of the human personality as an absolute value. Kant's justice demands that individuals conduct themselves according to a standard that is conceived as applying equally to all without exception. According to Kant, when individuals realize what is involved in the phenomenon of justice, they cannot help postulating their own equality as something fundamental.

Even though Marx's philosophy differs widely from Kant's, he, in his unique way, also depends on the absolute value of the human being. He stresses the fundamental sameness among individuals. For those who are accustomed to associating distributive justice to Louis Blanc's classic statement: "From each according to his ability, to each according to his need" with Marxism, the linking of Marx to the principle of sameness will appear illogical.

That Marx is essentially opposed to distributive justice, however, is expressed in many of his writings. His polemic against Proudhon is a particular example of this. As for Louis Blanc's maxim, Marx only employed it once in his writing, suggesting its use only as a transitional device prior to the establishment of communism.

The chief purpose of the communist revolution is to destroy the unnatural division of labor in society, and to demonstrate the rejection of the validity of any distributive justice on the basis of "achievement." The classless society represents the negation of a distributive justice on the grounds of "ascription." In this manner, Marx implies that the connotative meaning of communist justice is the "overcoming of all dualism, and all contradiction" exposing the fundamental equality among human beings. Robert Tucker (1963) writes that:

> His [Marx's] philosophy expresses a search for unity - for a world beyond all antagonisms and therefore, beyond justice as equilibrium of them (325).

Hence, Marx contends that it is not the function of justice to eliminate the arbitrary inequalitites or to establish equilibrium. This is the function of the revolution. Without a thorough social reconstruction, justice is merely a self-serving ideological abstraction devoid of any real meaning.

There are other theorists who generally lean toward an Individual Autonomy justice and who emphasize sameness; but, who refute the degree of absolutism found in either the Kantian or Marxian variety. Stone (1965), for example, stresses sameness, noting that the only way one can truly comprehend the essence of the relationship between justice and equality is by appreciating the history of the settlements which have been made in the quest of justice; and by establishing the extent to which one can depend on the reliability of these settlements in the future (335).

And, Stapleton (1944) argues that a notion of justice which rests on a variability principle or disregards any "common human values" limits the significance of justice by undermining the interaction between individuals on a rational level. He stipulates that only in a conception of justice which attempts to guarantee "equal justice to all" can the natural diversity among individuals be allowed "most creative play" (113).

The Public Interest construct of justice generally consists of the notion of ordering human relationships in accordance with the common good. This construct of justice involves reconciling different and conflicting rights and duties with the principle of common good. The aim of justice, in this sense, is to rid society of any arbitrary elements, and to eliminate discrimination not grounded on relevant differences.

The Public Interest construct accepts a plurality of values and goals. It also accepts the possibility of conflict. The Public Interest perspective of justice is often associated with the questions of adjustment or balance. Another important feature of the construct, which may be inferred from the idea of maximizing interests, is the notion of distribution. In order to weigh the differences in terms of relevance or irrelevance, it is important to figure in either the ascriptive characteristics, or the achievement characteristics of all the parties involved. There are a variety of ways the differential principle is expressed in the theories of justice which approximate the Public Interest construct of justice.

Proudhon's theory of justice, for example, is linked to a distributive orientation. Proudhon's theory of "mutualism" is grounded on a reciprocal equality, an exchange of services. In his theory, Proudhon sought to shift the emphasis in distributive justice away from ascription over to achievement. Proudhon had a profound influence on the socialist movement throughout Europe. The idea of mutualism eventually evolved into the notion of "fair distribution of the proceeds of labor." Marx, of course, waged a battle against this with his tacit remark: "What is fair distribution?" (Marx & Engels, 1951)

All sorts of definitions or formulas of "fair" or proportional are proposed by numerous writers throughout history. Of the contemporaries, Ginsberg (1963), for instance, suggests that the formal requirement of justice is to assure that "like cases should be treated in a like manner." He proposese a "principle of proportionate equality" in the following rule:

> If differences are justified on the ground of relevant differences of the claims, the allocation should be proportionate to the differences. Where the differences cannot be estimated with precision, it is generally held that it is right to assure a minimum for all people and perhaps to see to it that

differential rewards do not endanger the minimum ... (79).

Rawls's (1971) "justice as fairness" is another example of a contemporary expression of the relationship between a general conception of justice and the "difference principle" of equity. He states his position in the following manner:

> Social and economic inequalities are to be arranged so that they are both (a) to the greatest benefit of the least advantaged and (b) attached to offices and positions open to all under conditions of fair equality of opportunity (83).

Rawl's "conditions of fair equality" is essentially a notion cf mutual benefit. He favors a differential principle on the ultimate criterion of performance or achievement. He suggests that sameness of treatment requires no restrictions "upon what grounds may be offered to justify inequalities" (507-511). According to Rawls, the consistent application of "giving justice to those who can give justice in return" assures that individuals are judged independently of their social status (511). He further claims that his notion of "justice as fairness" not only expresses the principle of reciprocity "at the highest level", but, it cannot be subjected to the objections leveled against arbitrary or even relative equality (507-511).

A justification of a distributive sense of justice has also been stated with reference to the potentiality of realization. De Tourtoulon contends that to reject equality in justice on the grounds that it is indeterminate, is to deal with the problem superficially. Depending mostly on a notion of limits, he claims that the various expressions of equality in a justice concept are not logically contradictory. They are essentially similar, suggesting that the distinction can only be made in terms of "potentialities". He writes:

> ...There are so many points that, taken on an abscissa whose limit is 'perfect equality', come nearer and nearer to the ordinate constituted by the 'potentiality of being realized' (Perelman, 1963: 11-12).

De Tourtoulon (1963) prefers partial justice, noting that complete equality of treatment is impossible to realize. All formulations represent no more than imperfect attempts to reach various limits of equality in order to obtain justice. He argues that the approximation of justice increases when there is no dependence on any ideal or infinite limit. At least there is success in a partial sense.

That the dimension of equality is indeed crucial to the problem of justice will be denied by none. But as long as the definitions of equality fall short of simultaneously accounting for the variablity of humankind and the disclosure of some core of consensus, a just resolution will become vulnerable to turning into an injustice.

B. Inter-Personal Subjectivity versus Impersonal Objectivity

Impartiality is another very important and popularly discussed idea associated with the concept of justice. Although, in some ways, impartiality is very close to the idea of equality, there are critical distinctions. Symbolically, impartiality as an element of justice has been represented by a virgin suggesting incorruptability, or by a blindfold signifying objective consideration. Of course, the symbols would be especially undesirable if they denoted lack of insight or intelligent and informed judgment. The precise expression of impartiality, however, in theories of justice has been the subject of great debate. Inter-personal subjectivity and impersonal objectivity are intended to typify two alternative approaches to the problem of impartiality in justice.

On the one hand, the modes reflect the concern over whether the pursuit of justice should be oriented in terms of maximally generalized and objective norms; or in terms of the subjective nature or special circumstances. On the other hand, there is concern over the often underlined regard for norms of right and wrong behavior as absolute (i.e., applying a single social norm to a complex situation ignoring other competing social definitions of rightness), and the practice of judicious situationalism (i.e., accounting for all the facts in particular circumstances). The judicial procedure in the English legal system, for example, has been generally developed on the belief that formality of procedure through the elimination of personal bias brings justice. Judicial ignorance and the impersonal quality of the judge are considered to be fundamental to justice under this system.

The English system is in direct contrast to the arbitration or conciliation which, for example, is characteristic of the procedure for settling disputes in many peasant communities such as India, Indonesia, West Africa, to name a few. Arbitrators are generally selected for their acquaintance with all the issues and the parties who are involved. This individual is usually an active member of the community in which the problems occur. He/she does not hold any special position of esteem as in the case of the English judge. Moreover, the

70

arbitrators are fully aware of the personal veracity of the individuals involved. They have full knowledge of how the circumstances developed. The role of the arbitrators is to make full use of all the knowledge in order to come to a settlement.

Both systems seem to exhibit special problems. Impartiality, in the sense of absolutism, may lead to an unfair disposition because certain facts are disregarded. There is a danger in the latter example of the case being decided on a political basis, in the sense that certain information or the power of certain parties may be given undue regard.

Inter-personal subjectivity of the sort illustrated by the example of arbitrators and impersonal objectivity which is represented by the English case have their roots in a variety of contexts. The pair of ideas can be related to several associative concepts. Julius Stone (1965, 1966), for instance, poses the dilemma in terms of particularism versus generalization. Eckhoff (1974) also begins his discussion by asking whether a decision of justice is based on "general rules" and principles, or whether it is based on an evaluation of "each individual allocation situation separately" (268). Then, he moves to establishing a relationship similar to substantive versus procedural reasoning.

Eckhoff writes that the substantive considerations suggest an expansion of the "spectrum of relevant premises" with the intent of gaining a "relatively comprehensive picture of both the factual conditions" and the probable end results of any particular decision (265). He considers procedural reasoning in terms of "limiting the scope of what is taken into account" and the exercise of general "restraint".

Homans (1961) also raises this problem of impartiality. He suggests, however, that the choice must depend on the "decision-making costs" which may be involved (81-82).

Justice according to the Normative Conformity construct is claimed to be neither personal nor transpersonal. It is expressly this quality of impersonality which gives rise to its claim of objectivity. Ross (1959) and Stevenson (1944), for example, are suspicious of any non-legal definition of justice, since otherwise it is believed impossible to distinguish the emotional from the objective (see Chapter Three). Impersonal objectivity is predicated on conformity to norms and laws and on the interaction based on them. The emphasis on impersonal objectivity suggests that what is just or unjust should be determinable at least in principle by all rational beings. This requires that the basis for the determination should be connected to a phenomenal social need, as order or peace, etc. The relevance of any consideration is dependent on its content, and not in the will or status of whoever puts it forward. Kelsen (1961) proposes the idea of <u>Grundnorm</u> which resembles Kant's notion of the categorical imperative.

With a Normative Conformity perspective of justice the judge must only consider the features of a situation which are relevant in the law. In this sense, impersonal objectivity is linked with the notion of sameness in that all individuals should be dealt with similarly with the burden of proof on those who would refute the similarity. It is not the judge's responsibility to establish impartiality. It is the judge's role to consider the modes of inequality or impartiality only in terms of relevance to the issues. In other words, when the impersonal objectivity is emphasized, it follows, that in a most important sense, individuals are the same.

Impersonal objectivity is also logically implied in the Individual Autonomy construct of justice. For example, impersonal objectivity is suggested in Kant's categorical imperative with the implication that there is a general and minimal basis for discriminating just activity. Kant stipulates that the formal character of morality implies certain behavior which is required by any ethic, and is basic to a phenomenal conception of justice. The inference is that minimal humanism is naturally and universally constructed by the use of reason.

The Individual Autonomy conception of justice rests on extending primacy to certain general values or rules which may be maximally or broadly applied. The claim for impersonal objectivity, then, has a definite transcendental quality. It states essentially that principles of justice must be regarded as possible, otherwise it is felt that no conception of justice is even feasible. From this view, justice is sought for the purpose of establishing some ground on which individuals may be judged.

The Public Interest construct of justice, however, depends more on the notion of judicious situationalism. This general position suggests that an "impartial sympathetic spectator" is an adequate interpretation of impartiality. Rawls (1958) insists that it is a mistake to equate impersonality with impartiality. Justice, in the sense of inter-personal subjectivity, requires that individuals should put themselves in the place of a "compassionate observer" of the human condition and should be disposed of any personal prejudice (186).

The meaning of impartiality, in this sense, culminates with the idea that the various interests in a conflict will be recognized with all the specifics weighed. The decisions or actions must be equitable, taking into account all the information presented. There are no standard rules to depend on for a decision of justice. The facts of the particular circumstances provide the information necessary for a just resolution. The allocation of priority, then, is directed to values which refer to specific individual or societal conditions.

Finally, the dilemma of impartiality is stated either in terms of: (1) Inter-personal subjectivity as demonstrated in views of justice generally ascribing to Public Interest Justice; (2) Impersonal objectivity which is stressed in both the Normative Conformity or Individual Autonomy constructs of justice. Impartiality in justice revolves around the quesiton of whether the specific effects of a decision or the general effects are considered.

C. Improvement versus Stability

The question of social change interjects innumerable awkward and intransigent issues in most theories of justice. At the threshold of the problem is the intractable incongruity between the concept of justice, and the unrelenting reality of social change. The question is whether the phenomenal meaning of justice is incompatible with such reality as intentional economic stimulation, deliberate social manipulation, the meditated redirection of demands, or the general restraint through the means of social control? The impending circularities of social change often experienced in the history of societies tend to block a full appreciation of the social processes inherent in the working out of justice. The modes of interaction and the cultural and historical inflections often depicted in certain personal resolutions of justice demonstrate the cognizance of both values and norms so deeply embedded in social processes and individual psychological attitudes. In spite of the attending complication presented by social change, justice demands the specification of the goals of social change. Two recurring themes of change may be found in the literature on justice: improvement and stability.

The pair suggest the dilemma between the possibility of benefiting from the demands of impulse and the immediate attention to social needs, versus the possibility of benefiting from general restraint and discipline. The latter mode of change expresses a justification in terms of safeguarding a particular social order from any temporary digression or some transitory demands. The former brand of justification depends on the occasion of opportunity or spontaneity to bring about some sort of social improvement. Of course, the connotation of spontaneity intended here[9] is in the natural and best sense of activity or self-control. Support for human spontaneity suggests that it "is presupposed by the law, and ignores all the authoritative directions coming from the law". It generally ignores "the lower and selfish desires with which the law must deal" (Faulkner, 1972: 84). The poet Euripides makes the connection between justice and spontaneity when he writes: "In justice is all virtue found in sum, and its activity in apparent perfect spontaneity" (104).

The various theories of justice which generally espouse an inclination to the idea of improvement usually demonstrate attitudes which are open to the possibility of experimentation and innovation, and are not enamored of tradition. Moreover, there is frequently revealed a great confidence in the human capacity for reason and humanitarianism. The problem of human progress is among the focal concerns of justice considered in this context. The themes which are often related to the possibility of improvement include the enhancement of individual freedom or the enlargement of the individual's rational control over social life, technological advancement, and a general alleviation of conflict in human life. In other words, making improvement a goal of justice entails taking as the major problem of modern society the achievement of liberty and individual responsibility in a world that requires the co-ordination of many millions of people in a pluralistic society. It suggests making full use of modern knowledge and technology. The challenge of justice is to reconcile individual freedom with wide spread interdependence.

A theory of justice stressing stability, however, usually suggests a less optimistic view of humankind. It often points to the enormous cruelties and irrationalities which are evident in political and social history. With the possibility that advanced knowledge can be used as easily for destruction as for the improvement of humankind, every accomplishment in the name of progress also denotes an occasion for an even greater atrocity. The general attitudinal predisposition toward a preference for the status-quo and respect for the past are consonant with this basic perspective, with the thrust of the orientation being not to protect the individual from the arbitrary interference of the state. Rather, the emphasis is on safeguarding the weak against the strong, and the state against instability and insubordination. The focus is on those values and institutions that have been developed and approved by history and on their capacity to move toward progress through the operation of a selective historical intelligence. There is less weight given to any current creative intelligence.

The literature suggests that the theories of justice which appear to favor a Normative Conformity construct of justice generally demonstrate a concern for stability. However, the theories which appraoch either the Public Interest or Individual

74

Autonomy constructs of justice seem to exhibit a preference for improvement.

One of the unique features of the Normative Conformity construct of justice is the concern for stability. When seventeenth century England was torn by civil war, Thomas Hobbes placed individual security and peace above everything else. In the twentieth century when wars and social disaster seem to increase rather than to diminish, many writers of justice reject the optimism that civilization is always advancing. To these theorists the fact that civilizations can die indicates that there is no necessity, and, hence, no justice in the sense of any notion of continuous social advancement. Theories of justice which express a reliance on improvement are criticized as representing mere idealistic rubbish, bound up with various transitory conditions of history and cultures.

Since science and technology furnish the principle inspiration and support for the notion of social improvement and continue to exist and flourish, and since the idea of progress has not been destroyed, suggests to some writers (i.e., Kelsen (1961), Austin (1954), Stevenson (1944), Perelman (1967), and others) a methodology to investigate its original premise. This methodology includes, among other things, the value of "objectivity". Accordingly, the search for an "objective" definition of justice ensues.

For Stevenson (1944) and Austin (1954), for example, objective regulation which assures order and the preservation of certain common values are perhaps at the heart of their notion of justice. When the question of justice is eminent, the resolution, in this sense, centers around the recognized social order implied in positive law.

For a Normative Conformity construction of justice, an action or decision of justice must correspond with the pattern of expectations defined by the social order. To totally question or disregard the defined order is to ignore the objective premise on which justice, along these lines, is developed.

Theories which approximate the Normative Conformity construct of justice set a premium on stability, and usually enlist the formal system of rules and regulations to do the job of providing the criterion. The persistence of the idea of justice in the direction of Normative Conformity suggests that science and technology offer the promise of progress of human life, only if human beings are harnessed to foresight, intelligence, and order, and only if actions and decisions can be objectively evaluated.

The Public Interest construct of justice is predicated on a collective association in which various conflicting values may coexist, and on the common belief that optimal conditions for harmonious life can be attainable. The master principle of social well-being gives way to the notion of the maximization of rights, and this necessarily leads to delineation of personal interests for the benefit of the whole. Since the social well-being or collective good is difficult to determine absolutely, the position also denotes a collective effort in a perpetual pursuit of the general well-being. The justification is based on improving the general well-being of society.

The early utilitarians sought to define justice in terms of the happiness principle implying the maximization of the happiness for the society and not of each individual. A more contemporary approach to justice in this tradition seeks to enhance the expression of interests in a community or society, and to lessen the conflict (Ginsberg, 1956). Stammler (1925), for example, tries to equate individual goals with those of society. Improvement or happiness in the society leads to the improvement or happiness in the life of each individual.

Kohler (1914), Ihering (1913) and Pound (1968) all imply that justice is a phenomenal component of civilization. For these theorists progress in civilization is broadly defined as the maximization of individual control which is appropriate to the level of cultural sophistication.[10] Finally, since the notion of improvement suggests variability, a derivation of justice in this sense must assume an inherently dynamic form.

The Individual Autonomy construct of justice is also generally stated in terms of the idea of improvement. It is also an inherently dynamic model. The final judgment involving the question of justice is not left secure without the test of the value of the freedom of the individual, which is held above all else. Locke (1943, 1958) and Rousseau (1762), for instance, both value the freedom of the individual above everything, and argue that the concept of self-government is essential, if it is to be just and successful. The moral ideals of Kant are originally inspired by Rousseau; Kant's notion of justice also suggests improvement of society which is measured by the degree of freedom.

Kant (1959) attempts to prove that the free spontaneity of the human mind is key to comprehending what is known about society and nature in general. It is a notion of a world styled by the mind out of information derived from innate sources. What is critical in this idea is that when the mind discerns certain limitations to its present knowledge of justice, it simultaneously moves beyond those limitations and becomes aware of an improvement. Furthermore, not only do positive judgments of justice, but negative judgments involving the notion of injustice, have significant roles in the greater social awareness of what true justice means. Similarly, Kant conjectures that the phenomenon that appears inconsistent or inappropriate in a particular system serves to illuminate the essential characteristics of that system. The inconsistency gives rise to a fuller comprehension of things.

Kant implies that social knowledge expands fundamentally through negative phases as well as through positive ones. It is at this jucture that Kant actually anticipates a "dialectic or reason" but he fails to develop it. He suggests that all social knowledge such as that involving the concept of justice is part of a dialectical process. Ultimately, our experiences of justice and injustice merge to yield an ever more complete insight into ideal justice. Instead of a goal of progress, the process involving the acknowledgement of justice is a constitutional part of it. For the individual, then, finite experience suggests that progress is never completed. There are, indeed, phenomenal experiences of it. The more coherence or understanding that may be obtained from a world of random and conflicting information, the closer a social knowledge of absolutes is approximated. This synthesis implies the identification of justice with the reality of progress.

While Marx accepts the idea of the dialectic, he has his own vision of the process. According to Marx, social knowledge depends on the material conditions governing the individual's existence, especially the economic mode of production. Science and technology make it possible to meet human needs in different ways. New forms of production alter the tenor of human existence and affect social knowledge as well as social institutions. Thus, in Marx's view such notions as justice are apprehended through actual life in society, and cannot be assimilated solely through some innate reasoning process. Moreover, Marx suggests that an individual's freedom and worth depends upon the greater control over the economic determinates in social life. Only at this point can justice be understood. Marx rejects any concept of justice which implies that ideals are real. He rejects a notion of justice which relies on the status quo.

Each theory of justice contributes some perspective of social change and offers certain unique modes of comprehending the phenomena of change associated with justice. The theories also demonstrate certain common features. Despite the variability in approaches, the different theories of justice which can be broadly considered under the Normative Conformity construct are more inclined to emphasize the value of stability in their own formulations. In contrast, the variety of theories broadly linked with either the Public Interest or the Individual

Autonomy constructs of justice, despite all the complicated differences, still have in common some notion of improvement.

D. Other-consciousness versus Inner-consciousness

In all theories of justice there are implied "a necessary and fundamental attitude of consciousness" (Del Vecchio, 1952: 77). Most theories of justice immediately present themselves with the question of what or who is the object of the social discourse? Accordingly, theories of justice may be distinguished in the broadest sense by (1) appraising actions in terms of social consequences; and (2) considering the motive or inner spirit of the agent.

The first type of discourse suggests that a concept of justice depends on an "other" consciousness, involving rationality and objectivity based on a social framework. Justice, in this sense, rests on the voluntary subordination of private values to the common values shared by members of a community or society. This emphasis does not imply any exclusion of individual interests. Indeed, it is usually held that common valuation derives its legitimacy from individual acceptance. Justice which depends on an other-consciousness generally alludes to actions or decisions from the standpoint of the whole community or society. The focus is on the attending effects on the whole. A collective sensitivity provides the reference point for this type of definition of justice.

The second position supposes that justice cannot be judged entirely by externalities. Justice, in this sense, focuses on the individuals themselves and on the principle on which they propose to act. Justice must penetrate the superficial consequences of behavior and emphasize the inner character and motives of the individuals themselves. This means justice must go beyond the merely beneficial results of the governing principles. In inner-consciousness, social rationality is substituted by the cognitive apprehension of the individual rationality, with each subject representing a responsible agent. Moreover, inner-consciousness is not intended to evoke the notions of selfish or deviant behavior. Quite the contrary, the continuation of individuals as free beings depends on the continuation of a society in which individuals must socially co-ordinate their individuality. Justice which depends on inner-consciousness necessitates rational and socially sensitive behavior. What differentiates the inner-consciousness from other-consciousness is the express pursuit of maximizing the goal of human freedom within the limiting controls of social life. A conception of justice reflecting inner-consciousness is directed to the expansion of individual freedom. A formulation of justice in the sense of other-consciousness is concerned with the limitations themselves on human freedom which is an inherent feature of co-existence.

This pair of alternatives, involving the choice between other and inner mindedness, refers to one of the most recurring themes in the writing on justice. It represents, also, one of the most problematic issues for a theory of justice. The problem of inner or other-consciousness is noteworthy since it has been at the center of ethical reflection and social theorizing. Different levels of consciousness, historically and theoretically, have been identified in social literature as well as in the literature on justice. Sorokin (1937-1941) suggests that societies fluctuate from ideational, sensate, and idealistic social patterns. He contends that socio-cultural phenomena and consciousness are determined by certain pervasive themes or concerns which dominate a culture or a historical time frame.

Similarly, Stone (1965) submits that modern individualistic philosophies of justice appear primarily as reactions against "medieval universalism," "feudalism," and "the authority of the church". The shift to a collectivistic orientation in justice, however, he claims, is due to a growing aversion to the development of industrialization and the problems that accompany it (5). In a description of American culture: Riesman (1953) notes the shift from the "protestant ethic" or "inner-direction" to a "social ethic" or "other-direction."

The study of human interaction and economic development in human history is essentially an inquiry showing both the relationship of justice and the dualism in human nature. It exposes the dilemma of other-and-inner-consciousness. The concept of justice ultimately provides a view of the world. It describes the relationship between the individual and society. It suggests a morality in its final estimate of reality.

If we begin with the premise that the worth of an action or decision is to be judged by the extent to which an other-consciousness is exhibited, the definition of justice can proceed in various directions depending on the nature of the answer to the question: What are the consequences of a just resolution on the community or society as a whole? There are two main alternatives: First, an action or a decision may be judged "just" if it yields social order or public peace. Second, an action or a decision may be judged "just" if it results in the general well-being of the whole.

Theorists who are typically inclined to a Normative Conformity construction of justice value societal organization over and above individual expression. Hobbes, of course, having little faith in human creativity and pointing to the negative aspects of inner-consciousness, opted for an other-consciousness when he placed the social order and the sovereignty of the state at the top of his system. Radbruch (1950) suggests that justice can be nothing other than the idea of law. In this context, he expresses an other-consciousness orientation in terms of a "self-forgetting objectivity" (95-96). Similarly, Duguit (1918) bases his concept of justice on the idea of the "objective law", which he derives from the social facts linked with social solidarity and the collective conscience. Alf Ross (1959) also defines justice as conformity with existing law, and asserts that the only objective basis for a concept of justice inheres in its ability or efficiency of approximating an awareness of others.

It is generally argued by the supporters of a Normative Conformity perspective that an objective and rational justice cannot be derived from an inner-consciousness or from an exclusive awareness of the individual. Rather, only the cognition of others can lead to an objective notion of justice.

Implicit in the Public Interest construct of justice is the idea that the rational judgment involved in appreciating the notion of social benefit is not deducible from an inner-consciousness. The early utilitarians, for example, underscore the altruistic sensitivity when they advocate the pursuit of the "greatest happiness of the greatest number". The utilitarians found in altruism a principle which to them seemed superior to the self-interest of the individual. They base their altruistic principle on the argument that individuals desire happiness, and in order to find happiness, consequently, this means that all have an interest in general happiness or the happiness of others. The influence of the Christian ideal of selflessness may be particularly noted in mature utilitarianism. John Stuart Mill (1957) even attempts to identify the utilitarian ideal with that of "the Golden Rule of Jesus of Nazareth." Other theorists in this basic tradition have emphasized the advance from conflict to co-operation. The so-called social mindedness in human behavior served Herbert Spencer (1892) as evolutionary evidence supporting his basically hedonistic ethics.

Even when happiness is not the essential criterion of social utility, the other-consciousness is an elementary feature. Ihering, for instance, defines justice in terms of social interest, arguing that human coexistence "must be defined, as the actual organization of life for and through others" (Stone, 1965: 152). Finally, Holmes (e.g., 1897, 1927), representing a more recent preference for other-consciousness, maintains that the decision of justice may ultimately be reduced to questions of social policy and social advantage.

In both the Normative Conformity construct and the Public Interest construct there is a general dependence on the idea of other-consciousness as a dimension of justice. Accordingly, the other-consciousness is an inherent part of social reality which gives society its specificity and posits the notion that society is more than "the sum of its parts."

An Individual Autonomy construction of justice is unique on this dimension because it supposes an evaluation of an action or decision of justice in terms of its ability to co-ordinate the expression of one's capacities, and to the degree to which the fulfillment of the individual personality is attained. Following Kant's lead, Del Vecchio (1956) describes the inner-consciousness in justice by using his notion of "trans-subjective consciousness." The following passage illustrates this point aptly:

> For our task this principle above all must be firmly held: that there is a specific form of consciousness which we may call trans-subjective consciousness, through which the subject posits himself as an object in relation to others and recognizes himself as an element in a net of inter-relations between selves; that there is, in short an objective consciousness of self, whereby the subjective self becomes co-ordinated with other selves (80).

(underlined portions correspond
to author's own italics)

Stone's (1965) appeal to an inner-consciousness is made on another premise. Basically rejecting the idea that social interest must form the content of justice, he remarks:

> . . . the social interest is a name for the conclusion reached and not a method of reaching it (272).

In conclusion, the various constructs of justice appear to strike at the very core of human nature - a dualism which rises from a type of double existence: One seems to be rooted in the experience of the self; and, the second is derived from social experience. The pervasive difficulty of reconciling the inherent dualism in human nature with the content of justice often results in an arbitrary rather than a logical selection or empahsis of elements to describe justice. Durkheim (1973) warns that the "painful character" of this problematic may never be without tension. He writes:

> To the contrary, all evidence compels us to expect our effort in the struggle between the two beings

81

within us to increase with the growth of civilization (163).

Hence, far from attaining the level of predictability or resolution, this problematic which has been so widely treated in contemporary Western thought and notably in theories of justice, is consistently complicated by a world which is aggravated by the increasing complexity of modernization. The overwhelming extent of economic enterprise has engulfed and undermined the lives of a great portion of humankind. The harshness of the conflict of economic survival often seems to accent human veracity. More importantly it heightens the persistence of human beings toward fulfillment and self-expression. And, once the need for self-realization in daily social life is announced, the clash between other and inner-consciousness is pithily proclaimed: Will justice be held in account of the quality of social life with greater abundance of wealth and economic mastery, or will it be responsible for a more integral more expressive human being?

E. Perfectionism versus Practicality

When individuals deal with the problem of justice they are usually faced with the question of whether to emphasize ideals or facts. The question of the realization of justice in society often hedges on this dilemma. The history of justice suggests that this problematic has been broadly treated in terms of perfectionism and practicality. There are a variety of names which have been used to capture the general tenor of the relationship of meanings. For example, Stone (1965) broadly refers to the dilemma in terms of "metaphysical" and "empirist" criteria. Barry's "ideal-regarding" principles and "want-regarding" principles have similar implications (Stone, 1965: 288-299).

By perfectionism, the intent is to convey the idea that humankind is in a perpetual pursuit of the knowledge of universal justice or the most harmonious fulfillment of the human personality in society. The persistence of the search for social justice assumes that there may be a perfect justice. The notion of perfect justice is usually resolved to the belief that human beings, when given the opportunity, will strive by the most enlightened method at their disposal to establish the maximum of social justice (i.e., the idea that science will be used for the benefit of human beings). There is a general dependence upon the idea that the best or most positive qualities of humankind will ultimately dominate the lower activites and interests.

The implication of this is that the good life may be found in self-realization of justice. The expanding approximation of a universal reality is already partially expressed in every individual. For instance, when all the involved parties to a conflict over justice can agree on a reasonable and just resolution, a certain portion of the rational system of universal justice is exposed by finite reason. Sociologically, this implies a doctrine of symbolic relationships. That is to say, that the nature of social knowledge cannot be fully appreciated until these relationships are at least symbolically exhausted.

Since the moral value of justice is estimated by the contribution it makes to the harmonious perfection of all, the role of social participation and social institutions in the expression of justice is acknowledged. The self-realization of justice implies the increasing integration of human activity. The closer this is approached, the closer we come to the meaning of justice.

Subsequently, the theories of justice which lean toward perfectionism usually exhibit a great deal of energy deriving absolute type values, universal standards, a supreme good. The aim is to uncover the underlying principles of moral behavior without every paying too much attention to practical import. These types of theories are rarely identified with any particular set of practical issues or inquiries.

In contrast, theories of justice which are stated more in the practical sense usually contain a repudiation of anything as absolute, fixed or final either in human nature or society. Furthermore, there is generally a greater reliance on a more precise methodology, turned to the investigation of individual phenomena in terms of a more specialized type of inquiry into particular social problems. There is usually an emphasis on the immediately verifiable elements of life, as distinguished from the remote substance of the perfectionist perspective. The inquiries into justice according to a practicality emphasis are normally confined to the field of immediate experience. They rule out all idealism or utopianism of the sort propounded by perfectionism. Emphasis on practicality frequently appears somewhat less problematic, especially since it seems easier to identify human needs than to prove that whatever is just or real is fully intelligible. Theories of justice which attempt to associate social facts with the concept of justice attempt to inspire policy and decision-making with their perspective. Thus, there is a tendency to translate the meaning of justice in terms of doing or undoing. The end result is the reconstruction of mental experiences in the sense of mental adaptation to certain social facts. In this vein, there is a close connection to the premise that the justness of an act or decision is judged by its consequences and its ability to realize justice.

83

The theories of justice which are considered in the development of both the Normative Conformity and Public Interest constructs of justice appear to demonstrate a preference for the practicality dimension. The Individual Autonomy construct of justice, however, is unique, in that most of the theories which are included in its development broadly ascribe to a perfectionist point of view.

Most proponents of a Normative Conformity orientation customarily are skeptical of the effectiveness of the guarantee of certainty of any non-legal basis of justice. Since Normative Conformity justice is measured according to the consequences of human-social relationships on the public order and peace, it emphasizes criteria which provide proof of the practicality of attaining that goal. Radbruch (1950), for example, who argues that the notion of justice corresponds to the notion of law, suggests that "purpose conformity" is an essential part of the content of justice. Radbruch further contends that the association of justice with purpose conformity is intellectually impossible to derive from an "non-empirical" meaning of "purpose" (Stone, 1965: 245). Austin (1954) and Garlan (1941) agree that justice must be regarded in the sense of law, and they establish the element of practicality as the objective evaluatory aspect of justice. Similarly, Kelsen (1957) suggests that justice is best understood in terms of positive law. He asserts, however, that justice cannot be used to evaluate law. Instead the evaluatory function is assigned to the "principle of effectiveness." Kelsen writes:

> This norm may be formulated as follows: men ought to behave in conformity with a legal order only if this legal order as a whole is effective. No social order, not even the one we call "morality" or "justice", is considered to be valid if it is not to a certain extent effective, that is to say if the human behavior regulated by the order does not at all conform to it (224-290).

The theories of justice which typically contribute to the Public Interest construct also tend to stress a greater concern for the element of practicality. Justice depends on the degree of responsiveness to social needs, claims, and interests. Justice involves weighing competing values. Inquiries along this line of reasoning commonly necessitate the specification of the degree of competence of certain elements in the contest of certain conditions to sustain justice. It is not uncommon to find Public Interest type theories accompanied by various proposals or recommendations for certain public policies of justice.

In utilitarian proposals the idea of the "useful" or the "principle of utility" can only be understood in a practical context. And more specifically in Rawls' (1971) proposal of "justice as fairness", practicality plays an important role. He rejects the usefulness of perfectionism asserting that "Perfectionism is denied as a political principle" (329). Even though Rawls does not go the extent of denying the element of perfectionism, in justice, even as fairness, he concludes that "there is no evident need for a principle of perfectionism" (332). Generally, any idea of justice which rests on the notion of maximizing individual rights in a pluralistic society logically contradicts the idea of perfectionism.

The theories of justice, which have been considered in the development of the Individual Autonomy construct, seem to emanate from the criticism of the ethical insufficiency of any narrow or relative justice. Social values are generally evaluated and ordered to the extent that they support individual freedom and self-realization.

The classical Greeks sought to establish the supreme principle of valuation in a concept of justice. Plato put justice at the top of his hierarchy of values on the presumption that humankind will recognize it and let it dominate the lower values and interests. He believes that reason will ultimately control the emotional side of the human personality. In this way, Plato ties reason to the concept of justice. The right or the just decision is dependent on a rational intelligence. The classical quest for "highest good" thus evolves into a quest for the most prudent decision, and the organization of human values on this basis.

A more contemporary expression of this fundamental position may be found in T. H. Green's (1901) notion of justice. Green argues that human values are ordered in gradations according to (1) economic and material values which generally occupy a lower status; and (2) the spiritual values which are at the apex of the hierarchy of values. According to Green, it is the spiritual values which allow the full expression of the human being or the self-realization of the individual. He observes that values along the lower end of the continuum involve conflict and competition. Those at the higher end depend on co-operation and sharing for their attainment. Justice, in this system, is naturally the most important value for the self-realization of the individual. The more individuals share and co-operate, the closer they come to realizing justice, and ultimately, themselves.

A just resolution, then, in the sense of Individual Autonomy, suggests that the problematic inheres in the right choice and in the perfection of social values. It underscores the perennial question of perfectionism and practicality.

F. Sanctioned Duty versus Private Duty

Any conception of justice <u>not</u> only carries with it a pronouncement of certain values and a measure of action, it also indicates the conditions or extent of responsibility or obligation. The relationship between the content of justice and the element of obligation is also among the essential dimensions covered in the literature on justice. The obligation to act justly seems to derive from the ability of individuals to be influenced by certain judgments with regard to a particular conception of justice. Obviously, if a judgment or responsibility to act justly does not affect behavior in a desirable manner, there is no point in holding that person obligated by a particular criterion of justice. Exactly why a specific conception of justice is actually motivating is difficult to ascertain. There are no adequate methods for uncovering the processes underlying the sense of responsibility or obligation to behave justly.

The literature on justice appears to deal with the problematic insofar as we may distinguish between the external character of sanctioned duty and the internal character of private duty. Perelman (1963), for example, suggests that obligation is usually differentiated in terms of "juridical" and "ethical" duty. He describes the relationship in the following passage:

> . . . in ethics, there is freedom to choose the formula of justice that one intends to apply and the interpretation that one desires to give it. In law, the formula of justice is laid down, and its interpretation is made subject to the control of the highest court of the states.
> In ethics, the rule adopted is the result of the free adherence of the conscience. In law, it is necessary to consult the established order (25).

Similarly, John Ladd (1964) depicts this same relationship in his discussion of "externalism" versus "internalism". Alan Gerwirth's distinction between "act-morality" versus "agent-morality" is also comparable to the meaning intended by the relationship between sanctioned duty and private duty (1964).

An individual's duties may entail certain expectations for behavior by virtue of having committed oneself to a particular concept of justice. Duties, then, refer to the considerations

86

which guide and constrain rational choice in terms of a just resolution. The precise weight of such considerations depend on the nature of duties implied in a particular conception of justice, and on the degree of the individual commitment involved. For example, duties for individuals may be externally determined by the pattern of laws or the normative social order. Sanctioned duty and morality are fused in the social order established by society or the state. On the other hand, the idea that sanctioned duty and general morality must necessarily coincide, may be rejected on the grounds that obligation, in the sense of justice, must proceed from a notion of duty based on an inner kind of constraint. Here, the final measure of the decision to act justly ultimately lies with the individual, and inheres in one's own personal obligatory sense to act a certain way. Essentially, the query of this dimension is stated in terms of how wide a range of obligation should individuals expect when interacting with one another, when the problem of justice arises?

If the content of justice depends on the element of obligation, in the sense of sanctioned duty, attention is turned to reducing duty to a limited and clearly defined range of expectations. Such treatments of justice are usually restricted to the consideration of some objective and concrete criterion, and to a delineation of the conditioned aspects of obligation. The emphasis is on the authoritative nature of norms and laws, and the extent of the subtle obligatory force derived from them. Thus, the standard of a judgment involving the issue of justice is sought in the system of established laws or the normative social order.

Sanctioned duty presupposes a mode of decision-making that is motivated by a particular standard which is established either by custom or indicated by a formal set of guidelines. The idea of an immediate sense of duty or of what is right is rejected. Duty and, consequently, justice, is simply the culmination of denotative experiences underlying human behavior. This view suggests that the normative social order manifests certain intrinsic obligatory norms, and that only these norms can provide an objective study of the obligatory element in justice. The focus is more on the objective nature of action, rather than on the subjective nature of the agent. Finally, this orientation supposes that the scope of justice is to establish an objective order among individuals.

In contrast, theories which focus on private duty usually cover a broad and undefined range of expectations. Such attempts frequently involve proving a connotative awareness of obligation and treating the encompassing features of morality. Duty, in this sense, alludes to an inward obligation to one's own conscience and spontaneity of thought. For example, when

87

a passerby approaches a lake and observes a child drowning, he/she may not be legally liable to risk his/her own life to save the child's. Yet an individual in the given situation may feel a certain sense of duty, which goes beyond the legal prescription, to save the child's life. Here, obligation cannot be derived merely on the basis of an external standard. The implication is that private duty must originate in the individual conscience, and from the principle on which an action or decision is considered. Given the above situation, it is not sufficient to save the life of the one child. The action should be motivated by the commitment to the idea that saving human life is the right thing to do; and that individuals ought to respect human life.

Private duty in justice is tied to the notion of rectitude and love. Individual uprightness and love of humanity underlie private duty and are at the core of many theories of justice. Tying justice to the individual love of humanity and the responsibility to uphold human dignity suggests that the motivation to act justly is derived without any extraneous pressure or influence, in the sense inferred from the idea of sanctioned duty. Weight is given to an inner sense of what is just, and what is right. It is argued that this is as obvious as the fact of moral nature.

Many writers on justice regard the legal context paradigmatic for a discussion of obligation in justice. Historically, the blending of what has otherwise been called legality and morality is initiated by the rejection of the theory of natural law as the foundation of political and legal institutions. Hobbes discounted morality all together as a political restraining force on the grounds that it is vague and does not provide the necessary restraint over individual self-serving impulses. Thus, perhaps, beginning with Hobbes, and including more recent expressions, such as those by Austin or Alf Ross, the sense of obligation in justice is viewed from the perspective of sanctioned duty where morality is reduced to legality. Alf Ross (1959) suggests that sanctioned duty is more appropriate for a concept of justice; since what differentiates it from private duty is that the idea of legal consciouness is specifically aimed at the social order, while private duty merely implies a one to one relationship. Ross (1959) writes the following:

> The legal consciousness is, like the sense of morality, a disinterested attitude of approval or disapproval toward a social norm. It differs from the sense of morality in that, unlike the latter, it does not concern the direct relations between man and man, but the social organized regulation of community life.

88

. . . Legal consciousness is to a certain extent determined by the existing legal order itself and in turn exercises an influence on the latter (369).

This basic orientation has even led some to go as far as to agree with F. H. Bradley (1971), that "for practical reasons we need make no distinction between responsibility and liability of punishment."

The quality of sanctioned duty inherent in norms or laws which makes us answerable for a discharge of obligation is unique to the Normative Conformity construct of justice. When the element of duty is stated formally, we are answerable legally. However, any established measure of extent to make or to regulate, whether it be in the form of laws or in the form of approved models or customs, may be regarded in the broader sense. Even in its latter or more extended version, duty from a Normative Conformity formulation of justice can only accommodate a narrow range of expectations. No norms or laws can possibly anticipate every combination or situation which may enter into a relationship.

Both the Public Interest and Individual Autonomy constructs of justice, each in their own way, demonstrate an emphasis on private duty. Private duty provides the basis for the obligatory element in justice.

The Public Interest construction of justice suggests the pursuit of a common good and the maximization of people's rights. It requires that people exercise individual restraint in the achievement of these goals. The Public Interest construct of justice implies that we are answerable to the collective. Striving for the common ends involves certain voluntary social actions or roles. It does not suppose any specific assignments in regulating their attainment. Roles, in this sense, work on the individual members of society or group, creating certain duties and rights, which are independent of the desires of the individuals, constituting the group or society. There is introduced the element of voluntary enforcement. Since individuals have to assume many roles in society, the principles underlying roles, in general, become the restraining factor, rather than any one role in itself. This, then, allows great latitude for the interpretation of the extent of our responsibilities in social life. Individual duties are symbolically implied, encompassing the vast scope of social relationships.

Rawls (1964) demands that the duty of "fair play" is an individual matter. He writes that "obligations are normally, the consequences of voluntary acts of persons" (4). Relying, generally, on McDougall's and Piaget's theories of moral development, Rawls (1971) demonstrates a preference for

89

private duty, in the sense implied here, for his own theory of justice. The first stage of moral development is the "morality of authority" which is very close to sanctioned duty. The "morality of association" is an intermediate stage implying the notion of duty associated with certain social roles. The final stage or "morality of principle" suggests the generalization of duties associated with the principles underlying social roles. Rawls writes:

> In conjecturing how this morality of principles might come about ..., we should note that the morality of association quite naturally leads up to a knowledge of the standards of justice. In a well-ordered society anyway not only do those standards define the public conception of justice, but citizens who take an interest in political affairs, and those holding legislative and judicial and other similar offices, are constantly required to apply and to interpret them (473).

In this way, Rawls approaches a conception of private duty in justice which is very close to the Kantian interpretation. Rawls further writes:

> Once a morality of principles is accepted, however, moral attitudes are no longer connected solely with the well-being and approval of particular individuals and groups, but are shaped by a conception of right chosen irrespective of these contingencies. Our moral sentiments display an independence from the accidental circumstances of our world . . . (475).

Finally, Rawls connects the principle of morality with a common love of humankind. In the following statement friendship and justice are correlated:

> It [sense of justice] supports those arrangements that enable everyone to express his common nature. Indeed, without a common or overlapping sense of justice civic friendship cannot exist. The desire to act justly is not, then, a form of blind obedience to arbitrary principles unrelated to rational aims (476).

The Individual Autonomy construct of justice also implies that an individual is dutiful to the extent that one can act out of love for humankind. It depends on the individual ability to treat other people with respect and not like some objects. But this position includes the idea that one is obligated to the extent that individuals can govern their own actions by

90

principles, which may be adopted by all human beings. Kant (1959) insists that an appreciation of private duty is acquired a priori. Kant believes that the quality of "right" in justice cannot be derived by deduction from the facts surrounding what people do or what they have done, when the issue of justice is raised. Innate knowledge of patterns and inner considerations of prudence are central to Kant's idea of duty. Moreover, his insistence that justice serves to express individual freedom is introduced in connection with the idea that an action is not just or moral if it is determined externally by the will of another (e.g., state, monarch, parent, friend, etc.). Following, without the determination of an individual's rationality and free will to act justly, justice is impossible in the Kantian sense. The regard is more for the principles underlying actions, and not for the justification of a particular judgment.

Del Vecchio (1956) bridges private duty in justice to the notion of "charity" by citing several thinkers on this issue:

> As was well said by Romagnosi, 'Justice without the moral urge of charity is a cold word' . . . . Similar ideas have been expressed by F. Del Rosso: 'Love of justice must grow into love of charity' . . . . (149)

When we are answerable to an individual conscience for a discharge of duty, as is implied in the Individual Autonomy construct of justice, there is a dependence on the notion of the love of humankind, and responsible and rational self-command. Duty focuses not on the limiting factors of a relationship but rather, more on the individual ability to "fulfill his best self." Therefore, duty is rendered symbolic meaning and has broad implications for ordering social relationships.

The literature on justice appears to support the idea that those theories which broadly approach a Normative Conformity construct of justice are generally unique in stressing sanctioned duty over private duty, as an essential component of justice. The theories which approximate either the Public Interest or Individual Autonomy constructs of justice both place the emphasis on private duty as the primary obligatory element associated with justice.

G. Summary

Investigation of the continuing debate over the meaning and the context of justice gives rise to the crystalization of certain value sets which influence various conceptions of justice. The three patterns of conceptual dimensions which have been presented in this chapter represent three of the most common types of approaches to justice. But what is of special significance is that any conceptualization of justice simultaneously gives rise to certain inherent sources of injustice. This information may be discovered by looking at the criticisms that various theorists posit against other theorists. No theory of justice goes unchallenged. Since a particular definition of justice necessitates the selection of certain values among alternatives, it inevitably entails forsaking the attractive features of the rejected alternatives and accepting the negative features of the chosen alternatives.

For example, consider the debate over the sameness versus diversity dimensions. If we were to hold individuals equal in some absolute sense, injustice may result from disregarding the characteristics which differentiate us. On the other hand, if relative equality underlies justice, the characteristics which we all have in common may be underplayed enough to create injustice. The contrasting values represented by the list of conceptual dimensions exhibit both positive and negative attributes.

The wide interpretations of the dimensions of justice demonstrate the inherent paradox of justice. This inherent paradox of justice is at the root of the problem of finding a universal definition. Ironically, the prospect of a higher and vaster achievement often presents us with the risk of a more stupendous failure. The present age manifests this aspect of civilization in global terms.

According to the system of the patterns of conceptual dimensions, described here, a specific conception of justice may be theoretically categorized. A certain pattern can be extracted from the literature on justice, to the extent that it is logically coherent and consistent with a particular set of assumptions regarding human nature and society. Theories of justice may be considered to approximate the Normative Conformity construction of justice if they demonstrate the following pattern of conceptual dimension: sameness, impersonal objectivity, stability, other-consciousness, practicality, and sanctioned duty. This pattern shares two focal points with the Individual Autonomy construct, including the general concern for sameness and impersonal objectivity. It also has in common two dimensions with the Public Interest construct, which consists of other-consciousness and practicality. But what is unique in the Normative Conformity construct of justice are the dimensions of stability and sanctioned duty (see Table Two).

Similarly, a Public Interest construction of justice shares two qualities with each of the other constructs; and, it exhibits two dimensions which are unique to it. As stated above, it emphasizes other-consciousness and practicality with the Normative Conformity perspective. It also focuses on the dimensions of improvement and private duty with the Individual Autonomy orientation. The specific expression of diversity and inter-personal subjectivity, however, serves to distinguish this pattern from the others. Thus, a Public Interest construct of justice consists of the following patterns of conceptual dimensions: diversity, inter-personal subjectivity, improvement, other-consciousness, practicality and private duty (see Table Three).

Utilizing the same system of organization, the Individual Autonomy construction of justice has in common the focal concerns for sameness and impersonal objectivity with Normative Conformity; and for improvement and private duty with the Public Interest perspective. However, the emphasis on inner-consciousness and perfectionism are unique to the Individual Autonomy construct of justice. In summary, then, this construct depends on: sameness, impersonal objectivity, improvement, inner-consciousness, perfectionism and private duty (see Table Four).

There are several complicating aspects of the system of conceptual dimensions introduced here. Theoretically, the conceptualization of an individual's notion of justice should coincide with some general pattern of justice (i.e., Normative Conformity, Public Interest, or Individual Autonomy). But such an assumption cannot be accepted without some further consideration. There may be instances when certain conceptions of justice do not correspond exactly to the system indicated here.

The question of fit is, perhaps, among the most crucial. The exceptions may be composed of one of the following categories of cases. First, there are treatments of the justice concept which generally try to survey the whole field - the orientation being encyclopedic in nature. Treatments of this variety rarely develop their own theories. Rather, they merely provide a commentary on other theories. It is often difficult to grasp the author's own position in its entire form. The focus is usually on a "slice" of some other theories. For this reason, this type of treatment may be difficult to relate to our conceptual scheme.

Secondly, there is the category of theoretical treatment which investigates only one particular aspect of the question. The authors may focus on one area, because it is of particular interest to them; or, perhaps, they give it special depth of analysis. For instance, there are cases where the authors just emphasize the distributive sense of justice, or they deal only with the issue of equality. Since the present conceptual scheme is developed for understanding the full implications of the concept of justice, the types of treatment which represent a narrow aspect are only applicable to a certain portion of the scheme.

Third, there may be instances where the positions on justice are designed to represent a compromise. These positions may be formed by taking the best from different types of theories, and by combining them to make a new blend. It is possible, then, that the pattern of dimensions of these compromise positions may not approach any one particular construct of justice.

Fourth, there may also be cases which do not fit the conceptual scheme because of a simple error in logic. Indeed, there are many instances where certain attitudes, even from the same person, logically conflict. We must consider the possible conditional elements which complicate the expectations based on the conceptual dimensions of justice. Some of the conditional elements may include judgments which are made according to only a fragment of a particular logical system. That is to say, the decision may be made on the basis of only a portion of an individual or institutional experience. When a judgment is based on only partial consideration, or is fragmentary, it may be at variance with the general conceptual scheme. For example, most Americans support democracy and accept human equality (in the sense of basic sameness) as fundamental to it; yet, at the same time, many of these supporters of democracy favor minority segregation.[11]

Finally, there is the issue of the level of maturity of a particular treatment of justice. It is generally presupposed, here, that the more mature the level of theory, the more likely it will include the full range of associated ideas. Therefore, the more mature the theory, the more likely the theory will correspond to the conceptual scheme.

Thus, there may not be perfect confirmation of the present logical system. It is, nonetheless, important to note some of the general ways that discussions of various conceptions of justice arrange themselves. After all, the sociology of knowledge studies the fragmentary, as well as the total, impact of social phenomena (Schutz, 1967). Most formulations of social phenomena, generally, constitute a precarious equilibrium, which includes many hierarchies of ideas that often demonstrate numerous strains in divergent directions. The present system allows the connection of variable ideas of justice with an objective logical structure. A system of

94

The Pattern of Conceptual Dimensions Associated with
Normative Conformity Construct of Justice

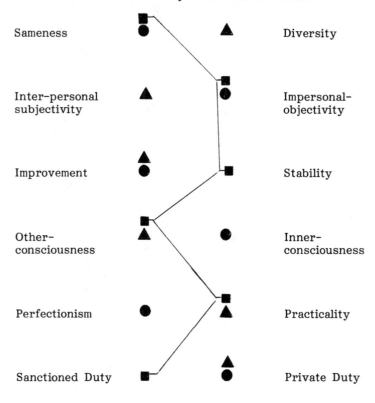

Sameness		Diversity
Inter-personal subjectivity		Impersonal-objectivity
Improvement		Stability
Other-consciousness		Inner-consciousness
Perfectionism		Practicality
Sanctioned Duty		Private Duty

■ = Normative Conformity

▲ = Public Interest

● = Individual Autonomy

Note: The Normative Conformity construct of justice shares with
the Public Interest construct a concern for other-consciousness
and practicality and with the Individual Autonomy an emphasis on
sameness and impersonal objectivity. The focus on stability and
sanctioned duty are unique to the Normative Conformity
construct.

TABLE THREE

The Pattern of the Conceptual Dimensions Associated with Public Interest Construct of Justice

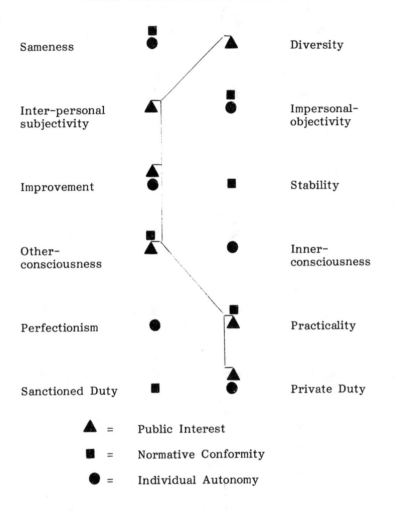

Sameness   Diversity

Inter-personal   Impersonal-
subjectivity   objectivity

Improvement   Stability

Other-   Inner-
consciousness   consciousness

Perfectionism   Practicality

Sanctioned Duty   Private Duty

▲ =   Public Interest

■ =   Normative Conformity

● =   Individual Autonomy

Note: The Public Interest construct of justice has in common with Normative Conformity the dimensions of other-consciousness and practicality, and with Individual Autonomy the dimensions of improvement and private duty. However, the Public Interest construct is unique in emphazing diversity and inter-personal subjectivity.

TABLE FOUR

The Pattern of the Conceptual Dimensions Associated with
Individual Autonomy Construct of Justice

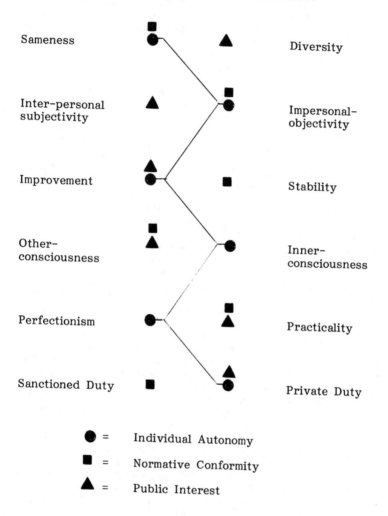

Note: The Individual Autonomy construct of justice shares
sameness and impersonal objectivity with Normative Conformity;
and, improvement and private duty with Public Interest. But
the concern for perfectionism and inner-consciousness is
particular to the Individual Autonomy construct of justice.

reference points which may be relevant to a fundamental definition of justice is implied. These reference points serve as a beginning for the categorization of social phenomena associated with justice. The conceptual dimensions of justice are designed to clarify and to differentiate the three constructs of justice. Further, the conceptual dimensions suggest points of emphasis on which the three modes of justice orient themselves. The conceptual dimensions serve to expose the dialectic, which moves between the idea of justice and the concrete expression of justice.

Another problem to be addressed concerns the completeness of the conceptual dimensions. On an intuitive level, the argument for inclusiveness depends on an account of what is essential to the meaning of justice. On an objective level we may hypothesize that if certain conceptual dimensions are necessary to a discourse on justice, we can expect to uncover these dimensions. There may be implicit or explicit themes as in grand theories of justice (allowing for fragmentary theorizing and logical inconsistencies). The latter has been more or less borne out by the literature on justice. The literature on justice generally supports the idea that certain conceptions of justice are accompanied by a specific rationality which considers particular sets of ideas or phenomena, rather than others. So far, the different forms of rationalization appear to demand the justification of their existence, and not so much of their inclusiveness. Until such proof is at least mentioned by someone in the literature, the problem of the possible omission of other dimensions is for now unwarranted.

But putting this consideration aside for a moment, let us account for the exclusion of certain ideas, which may appear seminal to the concept of justice. Perhaps, the most notable omission from the present list of conceptual dimensions is the apparent antithetical relationship between natural law and positive law. The exclusion is not based on the criterion of popularity or relevance to the theme of justice. Indeed, the issues are often central to certain concepts of justice. However, the problem exists because their implications are usually narrowly indicated. These conceptions are specific to a certain period of historical or theoretical development, and usually relate to particular schools of thought. The decision to omit this set of ideas is based on their inability to be applied to different concepts of justice, which represent different historical time frames. For example, the development of Individual Autonomy justice finds its roots in theories of justice which are based on the notion of natural law; but Individual Autonomy also includes certain more contemporary visions of justice, which are not dependent on natural laws theory. The construction is built on a broader spectrum of concern. If natural law, then, were a dimension, there would be many theories which could not be related to it. The basic assumption underlying this system suggests that the conceptual dimensions must be applicable to all phases of development of a concept, and to all types of treatment. The dimensions must have a sort of transcendental quality. Both natural law and positive law are appropriate only with references to certain philosophers. To this degree, they do not constitute general elements of the concept of justice.

The relationship between the sacred and the secular might also have been considered for the list of dimensions. But the exclusion is influenced by the fact that, whether a theory of justice is informed by some superior being or not, this quality does not form an inherent element of the meaning of justice. Yet any theory of justice, whether it be based on a sacred or secular criterion, may be related to all the dimensions listed.

Absolutism versus relativism is another set of antithetical concepts which is not treated directly in the present list of conceptual dimensions. This case is different from the others, because there is an effort made to treat the qualities of meaning, which are relevant to justice. For instance, the notion of relativism often refers to a refutation of any universals or standards. We may recall that this meaning can be found in both contexts of "diversity" and "practicality". On the other hand, by absolutism, the intention may be to describe the idea of a principle or standard, which underlies an unambiguous factor in the decision-making process, and which is to be applied at any time and in any place. We may remember that the shades of meaning captured under the dimensions of "sameness" and "impersonal objectivity" try to capture this within their specific contexts. The pair is not treated directly because, without the proper context, such terms as absolutism and relativism are "unanalyzed terms of censure and praise," which only lead to the complications, rather than the clarification of such a concept as justice (Fuller, 1954:457).

Another pair of ideas, relative to the concept of justice is determinism versus indeterminism. If justice is to be understood in the sense of a decision-making process, it must be considered within an indeterministic frame of reference. Kant suggests that concepts such as justice or ethics will be void of meaning, if they cannot be accompanied by the assumption that individuals have the ability to make rational choices. Most theorists, regardless of their particular conception of justice presume individual rationality and the ability of individuals to make rational decisions.

A case for indeterminism may be made on the basis of a sociological argument. Jacob, Flink and Schuchman (1962), for example, suggest that social norms are rarely transmitted with any degree of precision. In most instances, there is a great deal of room for interpretation and expression of various social norms. Furthermore, since the transmission of norms and values take place in the midst of constant change, they fall victim to constant re-evaluation and re-adjustment. This detracts from any precision in their communication. Arnold Rose (1962) contends that the levels of expectations are broadly formed on the basis of "role", and not on some exact delineation of behavior. This means that there is a great range of behaviors applicable to certain situations, allowing for a broad spectrum of choice. Accordingly, justice engages a great range of interpretations and suggests numerous forms of expressions. Therefore, it must essentially be viewed indeterministically.

Our overall effort has been to design the dimensions in such a manner that they are broad enough to incorporate many different forms of interpretation or other dimensions mentioned in the literature. While there are, of course, certain other ideas which could have been considered in the list of the dimensions, their infrequent appearance in the literature or their relatively limited suggestive power is deemed reason enough to exclude them at the present time. Only the most essential and popular ideas are included in the list of conceptual dimensions. Although the conceptual scheme is general enough to include other dimensions, the scheme cannot be subsumed by any other dimensions or lists.

Perhaps the most important problem facing the conceptual scheme involves the question of the application. Unless we can demonstrate the usefulness of the conceptual scheme, the justification of the components is not worth the effort. This problem is examined in the next Chapter.

Chapter Five

JUSTICE AND ABORTION

Traditionally, the main criticism of the concept of justice has been that it lacks pragmatic or predictive significance. The point of developing a conceptual scheme of justice is to render it some analytical power and applicability. The relative success, however, of such a system lies in its capacity to contribute to the understanding or resolution of some concrete social question concerning the justness of an action or decision.

The abortion dilemma has been selected to demonstrate how the conceptual scheme of justice developed in this research may be employed to understand the problem better. Few social problems are more extensive in scope, and combine both religious and secular justifications.

The question of justice in the abortion controversy is, at once, concerned with the nature of humankind and the role of society in the individual decision-making process. It also implies what the relationship between society and the individual ought to be in order that justice may be realized. Indeed, rarely is the meaning of justice and the implication for what it means to be a human being so deeply problematic.

Kamla Mankekar (1973) writes that "the practice of abortion is as old as civilization" (4). And George Devereux's (1960) comprehensive cross-cultural study provides proof that abortion is a known practice in most cultures. His investigation brings him to the opinion that:

> . . . abortion is an absolutely universal phenomenon and that it is impossible even to construct an imaginary social system in which no woman would ever at least feel impelled to abort (161).

While Devereux's findings are in themselves interesting, he goes even further in his analysis of the data, concluding that a number of indicators suggest, that where abortion does exist, there is a taboo against mentioning the subject.

The open concern over abortion is a relatively recent phenomenon. As late as 1936, one of the first comprehensive books on the topic was published in the United States. In it, Frederick Taussigh, the author, first states that "abortion has become a world problem."

Barbara Plant (1974) reviews the abortion literature in the Readers' Guide to Periodical Litereature from 1890 to 1970 and notes that only one article on abortion could be found prior to 1930. She suggests that the decades of the thirties and forties mark the beginning of literary interest in the abortion problem, with an increase of writing to 25 and 26 articles, respectively. The number of articles in the decade of the 1950's, numbering 42; and in the 1960's the index contained 180 articles, giving evidence of the great concern and openness which had developed.

We can find in the literature that there are substantive differences in the way the topic of abortion is treated during different time periods (See Ebaugh and Haney, 1980; Krannich, 1980; Cutler, et al., 1980; Jones and Westoff, 1978; Chesney & Lind, 1979; Eders and McGee, 1980; Tedrow and Mahoney, 1979). Books and articles appearing prior to 1960, usually seem more concerned with the nature and scope of the problem of abortion rather than with drumming up support to activate any social change. The literature of the 1960's may be distinguished by writers generally attempting to justify certain positions in order to convince readers of their claims. The literature of the 1970's, especially since 1973, similarly concentrates on pro- or anti-abortion issues with special emphasis on the Supreme Court decision (Roe v Wade) and its various interpretations. Much of the writing of this time seeks to either affirm the decision or have it reversed.

The more recent literature in the 1980's continues the argumentative style and demonstrates an even greater widening of concern. Abortion is often associated with such varied topics as: family planning, population control, sterilization, birth control, genocide, law, crime, taboos, sex roles, maternal deprivation or the unwanted child, the quality of life, and the sanctity of life. Furthermore, the arguments which characterize the abortion controversy have been variously approached. They have been expressed in the context of many different interests and inclinations - historical, economical, demographic, medical, moral, religious, sociological, psychological, and philosophical perspectives all having some role. With the Supreme Court's recent reaffirmation of Row v Wade on June 15, 1983, we will undoubtedly see a renewed vigor on the part of interest groups, e.g., anti-abortionists, to have the ruling overturned. In a 6-to-3 majority, the Justices overturned about two dozen state laws that had put a variety of restrictions on women seeking abortions. States may no longer require that all second trimester abortions take place in hospitals or impose a 24 hour waiting period before an abortion may be performed. The court also struck down provisions requiring a doctor to discuss the fetus as a "human life" and those requiring all teenage girls to get permission for an abortion from parents or judges (City of Akron v Akron 103 S. CT. 2481 (1983); Center for Reproductive Health, Inc. and Planned Parenthood v Ashcroft 103 S. CT. 2517 (1983)).

What is especially striking, and at the heart of this chapter, is that each type of justification (criterion), whether pro- or anti-abortion, in its own way attempts to appeal to some positive values of human dignity and social well-being. An opinion regarding the justness of abortion usually involves the reconciliation of the conflicting rights for freedom, with the limits of social control. Objectively, no single justification can be judged entirely negative. Most solutions to the problem seem to share in their motivation - the quest for justice. Hence, Callahan (1970) adds, that, "There would be no abortion debate if there had not been a gradual growth of moral consciousness" (8).

In order to make their respective points, however, all perspectives become vulnerable to the age old problem of bias and extremism. Wertheimer (1971) writes that, "ultimately, most liberals and conservatives are, in a sense, only extreme moderates" (89). Both ends along the continuum of contention alike assume responsible and rational behavior. In the contest with one another, however, both positions have become grossly complicated with irrelevant data, exaggerations, misconceptions, and inconsistencies. Thus, to merely develop more extreme consequences of certain arguments, or to attack the various proposals offered by those who are essentially trying to find just solutions to a critical human problem, may be fruitless and even irresponsible.

A systematic and controlled approach which establishes a common ground for comparison may be instrumental in the discovery of the objective sources of justice and injustice in the various perspectives on abortion. We propose, here, that the conceptual dimensions of justice can serve as the objective reference points for these comparisons. The degree to which the conceptual dimensions of justice are expressed in the different positions on abortion may underpin the fundamental definitions of justice underlying them.

The treatment first entails using the common dilemmas of justice to organize and form the basic composite positions in the abortion controversy. These dilemmas are then employed to obtain a meaningful relationship among the positions, and, in turn, to connect them with the constructs of justice. It is not the purpose of the present work to provide a distinct or new type of argument or conflict-resolution. Rather, the objective is to suggest a methodology, which may lead to a more efficient or effective approach for an understanding of the issue of justice in the abortion crisis. The greater implication here is that a similar technique can be employed to study the question of justice in the context of other social problems.

The immediate quandary involves the selection of the data or literature that would demonstrate the variety of ways justice may be expressed in the abortion controversy. The question is whether the consideration should take the works of a few renowned writers and compare their specific opposing views; or whether to develop some fundamental composite position portrayed by an adequate sampling of works published within a certain time frame? The latter course is taken here. A sample representing each type of solution proposed to the abortion dilemma which appeared roughly between 1965 and 1980, with the possible exception of some popularly cited works of an earlier period, is considered here.

A. Basic Positions in the Abortion Controversy

Many different types of categorizations describing the positions on abortion have been proposed in the literature. Some theorists/reviewers simply group the arguments in terms of either anti-abortion or pro-abortion sides (e.g., Sarvis and Rodman, 1974); and some, in terms of conservative or liberal proximity (e.g., Wertheimer, 1971; Sumner, 1974; 1981); or, in the sense of a traditionalist's and a reformer's standing (e.g., Kluge, 1975). Other authors seem to find it more convenient to organize their discussion of the issues in modes of three, as for example, the restrictive, moderate, and permissive viewpoints (e.g., Callahan, 1970; Grisez, 1970; and Brody, 1975). A more defined categorization plan has been suggested by John M. Finnis's (1970) "Three Schemes of Regulation":

(1) The 'rights of the child': strict criteria and expost control by criminal law;

(2) The 'rights of the medical profession': broader medical criteria and control by prior authorization.

(3) The 'rights of the woman': uncontrolled application of indeterminate (187-197).

Essentially, there are very few substantive differences among the classificatory proposals. To capture, in the most general sense possible, the variety of alternatives to the abortion problem, the following scheme is utilized:

(1) Anti-Abortion - with strict prohibitions to insure full commitment to the value of the sanctity of life.

(2) Pro-Abortion - with mild regulatory system to assure general well-being.

(3) Pro-Abortion - with no formal sanctioning to insure personal freedom of choice and general availability of service.

Of course, each model includes a rather wide spectrum of interpretation. For instance, the first model encompasses both the arguments which restrict abortions regardless of the circumstances, and those which allow rare exceptions. Different writers make different exceptions; but generally all hold fast to the idea that strict prohibitions are a necessary element. Thus, authors as varied as Brody (1975), Gardner (1972), Grisez (1970), Granfield (1969), Hilgers and Horan (1972), Kluge (1975), Noonan (1970) and Norman St. John-Stevas (1964) may be considered in light of the first model or position.

The range of arguments comprising the second model is also wide. In some cases the regulations are intended to imply a compromise which allows the state to safeguard the fetus only after it has reached a certain level of gestation. In other instances, the appeal for regulations is carried out in terms of the licensing statutes for medical personnel and facilities. To this end, James George (1967) refers to the "administrative sanctions." Finally, there are those who present a moral and legal policy whereby the abortion question can be "judiciously" formulated. Callahan (1970), Curran (1971), George (1967), and Wertheimer (1971) are among the writers who propose some sort of regulatory procedure and may be among those comprising the list of authors ascribing to the second position.

There is also wide span of opinions covered in the last model. Some prefer to consider "abortion on demand", while others favor the notion of "abortion on request". Still others attempt to disassociate abortion with any terms whatever. Hence, people who represent such diverse views as Guttmacher (1967), Hardin (1968, 1973), Lader (1967, 1973), Rossi (1966), and Szasz (1966) may be associated with the third alternative.

Having defined broadly what is meant by each model or position in the abortion controversy, attention may be directed to an examination of exactly how the conceptual dimensions of justice are expressed in these three positions. The major assumption, of course, is that the question of justice is central to the abortion dilemma.

B. The Relationship Between the Conceptual
Dimensions of Justice and
Issues of the Abortion Controversy

Sameness versus Diversity

Justice is often symbolized by scales suggesting balance. Aristotle observed that "all men hold that justice is some kind of equity." Controversy exists over what the principle of equity should be based upon. Should the similarities or the differences among human beings be taken into account?

Justice resting on sameness depends on the success of establishing some common features among human beings and demonstrating the irrelevance of certain differences. The problem is to provide a basis for justifying equal treatment. Justice, in this sense, consists of rendering to every individual the exact measure of his/her dues, without regard for any personal worth or merits. All individuals are placed on a horizontal plane.

Justice in this way seeks to eliminate special privileges based upon unwarranted or exaggerated power or status. The demand of justice is to extend fundamental rights to all groups or all types of individuals irrespective of their differences. To this end: "Justice is the effort of man to repair the inequality of nature" (Kelly, 1900).

Justice which takes into account the diversity among human beings must defend the relevance of the differences which are under scrutiny. Not all individuals are considered equally deserving or equally blameworthy. Justice discriminates between individuals, observing a "just" proportion and comparison. Individuals are placed on a vertical plane. Two general categories of distinctions may be considered in a justification based on the diversity principle: The first takes into account the variable of social position including such variables as age, sex, class, etc. The second source of distinctions is based on social achievement.

The unique question in the abortion controversy which may be directly related to the sameness versus diversity dimension asks: what regard must be given to the unborn fetus: Or, in the words of Szasz:

> The question is: What is abortion - murder of the fetus; or removal of a piece of tissue from the woman's body? (1966: 148)

Germain Grisez (1970) suggests that there are three alternatives to this query: First, the fetus may, from the moment of conception, be consistently assigned a "person status". In which case an intense moral issue is raised. The latest Supreme Court ruling, as we noted, addressed this issue in their 1983 session. They ruled that physicians were not required to refer to the fetus as "a human life". Second, the fetus may be consistently valued as a "non person." In which case the most appropriate treatment of the unborn is as part of the mother's body. This position denies human status to the conceptus. Lastly, the fetus may be considered in the sense of both of the above alternatives. That is to say, that up to a certain period in the pregnancy, the fetus may be consistently given a "non-person" status; and, afterwards, it may be consistently regarded as a person. In the last position, the differences in the developmental stages are emphasized. Since the stages ultimately depict human development, the position suggests, in the least terms, that the conceptus is more than a mere "piece of tissue" (Sarvis & Rodman, 1974: 410).

The anti-abortion proponents generally seek to justify their position by assigning a "person" status to the fetus. The fetus is said to have "its own autonomy, its own brain, its own nervous system, its own blood circulation" (Barth, 1982: 92). Arguments for this position vary from the non-scientific to the relatively more sophisticated (Solomon, 1980; Gustafson, 1982; Harrison, 1982; Curran, 1982; Prager, 1981; Smith, 1981). Another approach is to converge on the similarities or sameness among the stages of development in which it is claimed that there is essentially no difference between a "zygote, embryo, fetus, infant or senior citizen" (Sarvis & Rodman, 1974: 21). All forms of human life deserve equal protection (See Sumner, 1981: 89). Therefore, to condone the destruction of any one stage of development would be equally wrong or immoral. David Granfield (1969) expresses this idea when he writes:

...abortion is a use of power by one human being over another: It established a drastic inequality (124).

David Louisall and John Noonan (1970) maintain that as the level of knowledge and technology reach greater sophistication the arbitrary points of development in the womb will become less pronounced. Similarly, the science reporter for _Life_, Albert Rosenfeld (1969), states:

Many readers of _Life_ [1965] who saw Lennart Nilson's marvelous photographs of fetuses in their sacs, especially in the later stages of development, wrote in to say that they could never again think of their babies as disposable things. Such sentiments might well increase as fetuses become visible from the outset (125-126).

Cooke, Hellegers, Hoyt and Richardson (1968), in The Terrible Choice - The Abortion Dilemma, add that -

> Even the most accurate knowledge of the fetus cannot answer what value each stage of development has for society, for the mother or father, or in religious terms, for God (39).

The fact that the fetus is human (i.e., at least potentially a person), generally provides the basis for the common acceptance of the fetus as a person (Fletcher, 1982). Equal justice for the fetus is, therefore, demanded on this ground.

The advocates for pro-abortion with no restrictions also generally indicate an interest in justice based on the sameness principle. However, the two positions differ in their interpretation of this.

First, the supporters of the pro-abortion with no restrictions consistently deny "person" status to the fetus. Garrett Hardin (1972), the renowned biologists, says:

> Whether the fetus is or is not a human being is a matter of definition, not fact; and we can define any way we wish in terms of the human problem involved, it would be unwise to define the fetus as human.
>
> . . . .
>
> Abortion-prohibitionists generally insist that abortion is murder, and that an embryo is a person; but no state or nation, as far as I know, requires that the dead fetus be treated like a dead person (169).

Similarly, the Honorable Holmes (1970) in the case of Dietrich argues that the unborn child is part of its mother, and that in the law there must be a certain amount of arbitrariness (Dietrich versus Northampton, 138 Mass. 14, 52 Am. Rep. 242 1884). By denying "Person" status to the fetus and regarding it only as part of the mother's body, the focus is placed entirely on the woman. Justice, in this sense, is not sought on behalf of the fetus. Rather, it is the woman who deserves equal treatment under the law.

To this end, the American Civil Liberties Union (A.C.L.U.) rejects prohibitive abortion laws because they . . .

deny the women in the lower economic groups the equal protection of the laws guaranteed by the Fourteenth Amendment, since abortions are now freely available to the rich but forbidden to the poor (1970: 27).

In a keynote address before the California Conference on abortion, Senator Maurine Neuberger (1971) adds:

The code satisfies few and discriminates against many... We have only to look at the statistics in Catholic countries to know that there is a vast discrepancy between practice and doctrine (111-112).

In the same vein, Edwin Schur (1964) suggests that abortion is so widespread, this in itself provides support that a great number of women in the United States want equal control over their personal bodies, and desire the equal right to decide whether or not to have children. (See Hansen, 1976; Naumann and McDianmid, 1981) Schur argues that:

laws against abortion may well serve to further women's subservient social status (376).

Thus, the general contention is that the anti-abortion laws are not equitable or consistent in their application to women. For this reason, they provide an inadequate standard for justice.

The different interpretations regarding the human status of the fetus appear irreconcilable. The many confrontations - the absolute right of the fetus versus the absolute right of the woman - attest to that fact. This may have caused some individuals to consider the "differential" principle (diversity) in the formulation of justice.

The problem of human development usually entails the use of numerous names by which we may refer to the different stages of prenatal life. These include: conceptus, fertilized ovum, body tissue, zygote, embryo, fetus, prenatal infant, unborn child, etc. The technical distinctions are often difficult to establish. The words serve as reference points for the emotional and intellectual definitions for the onset of life. Typically, the beginning of life or "person" status is marked according to a certain time or stage of development as conception, quickening, viability, birth, or achievement.

Knutson notes in his studies that those individuals who ascribe to religious and biological definitions of when life starts usually employ earlier times or stages of development. Those

109

individuals who regard soiological, cultural or psychological definitions usually tend to refer to the later stages of development. Knutson also finds that women usually tend to fix the beginning of life according to biological definitions. Men more often tend to be attracted to the factor of independence from the mother or to the personality and sociocultural considerations (Callahan, 1970:350). He concludes that different lines of demarcation are frequently contrary to the legal and institutional definitions. He suggests that the lack of consensus fosters numerous personal and professional conflicts between values and obligation.

Many individuals stress the potentiality of the conceptus to develop into a human being. They do not try to equate it with the human person or to deny its value altogether. The pro-abortion with regulation position stems from this middle orientation. It implies that while the precise person status of the fetus is indeterminable objectively, its special quality of human does not allow the arbitrary decision to merely dispose of it at any time or in any manner whatever. Wertheimer (1974) summarizes this position:

> The fetus is not a human being, but it's not a mere maternal appendage either; its a human fetus, and it has a separate moral status just as animals do. A fetus is not an object that we can treat however we wish, but neither is it a person whom we must treat as we would wish to be treated in return. Thus, some legal prohibitions on abortion might be justified in the name of the fetus qua human fetus . . . . (45)

There are varying degrees of regulation proposed by the writers, who may generally ascribe to the pro-abortion with regulation position. But as the name of the position suggests, there is no inclination to prohibit abortions. Wertheimer (1974) points to the limitations of this position:

> It does not show that abortions are morally okay; at best it shows that the legal prohibitions are not. Nor does it work against every possible prohibition of abortion; statutes having milder social liabilities might be warranted without arguing for the fetus' humanity (50).

The different periods of gestation must be given special consideration. The closer the fetus is to human form (birth) the more rights it has and the more protection it is afforded by society. This formulation of justice takes into account the relative inequities, and the differential opportunities of the various parties of the argument to exercise their rights. In this sense, justice is derived through the maximization of rights.

"Sameness versus diversity" represent two mutually incompatible values of justice. The dialectical relationship between the positive and the negative features of these values is problematic for the concept of justice. The acceptance of either one implies the simultaneous conditions of justice and injustice. Recalling Aristotle's cogent expression of this dilemma: "Injustice arises when equals are treated unequally and also when unequals are treated equally."

Interpersonal Subjectivity versus Inpersonal Objectivity

Impartiality, which is commonly linked with justice, is symbolically represented by a virgin suggesting incorruptibility and a blindfold signifying objective consideration. Formality of procedure, and the impersonal quality of judges are considered to be fundamental to justice. But no one intended judges to be ignorant of the facts. In addition to being objective, they are to act as arbitrators making full use of all the knowledge in order to come to a just decision. The question here is whether an evaluation of the justness of a decision or an action is based on maximally generalized terms, impersonal objectivity, or in specific circumstantial terms, inter-personal subjectivity. In legal jargon the meaning intended by the pair of conceptual dimensions may be captured within the definitions of procedural versus substantive reasoning, respectively. Substantive justice suggests a greater scope of relevant information, aiming to be relatively comprehensive in its formulation. A more narrow spectrum (i.e., general restraint) and the success of applyig general rules are elementary to a procedural formulation of justice. Depending on the point of emphasis special problems for the concept of justice are indicated.

Maximizing objectivity may lead to an injustice because certain facts are disregarded or missed. By maximizing circumstantial or substantive issues (subjectivity) there is danger of the case being decided upon bias.

Neither the pro-abortion without restrictions nor the anti-abortion advocates, deem it logically feasible, either in the moral or the legal sense, to acknowledge any ground on which abortion can be justified or not (whatever the case may be) for certain indications. The anti-abortion stance, generally, cannot justify abortion for any reason. The believers of pro-abortion with no restrictions insist that there should be no need for any special justification of abortion at all.

111

Robert Drinan, S.J., (1970) represents many anti-abortionists when he demonstrates his opposition to the Model Penal Code. The Code suggests the revision of the laws in cases of rape, incest, and considerations of eugenics, and maternal mental and physical health. According to the Code, "deadly force may be used to defend oneself against death, serious bodily harm, rape or kidnapping" (ALI Model Penal Code 3.04(2)(b), 1962). The question raised is whether in areas where the risk to the woman's life is minimal, the burdens of pregnancy and childbirth can be compared to either serious bodily harm or to rape. While the Code does not define "serious bodily harm", it does define "serious bodily injury", which it uses in analogous contexts, as a "substantial risk of death or which causes serious, permanent, disfigurement, or protracted loss or impairment of the function of any bodily member or organ" (ALI Model Penal Code 210.0(3), 1982). It is argued by proponents of the Code that the woman suffering from a pregnancy (assumedly an unwanted pregnancy) experiences, then, a protracted impairment of function of her body as a whole," (Regan, 1980: 48). Drinan, obviously disregarding this interpretation, rejects the Code on the following premise:

> The Model Penal Code puts into operation for the first time in American law the concept that the state may grant the individuals the right to terminate a life which is inconvenient for these particular individuals (22).

Most advocates of the anti-abortion stance press for an impersonal objectivity, or, the unqualified protection of the fetus. They assert that extending the scope of the problem to include special circumstances merely serves to muddle and undermine the fundamental issue. For the opponents of abortion, revised or less restrictive laws are inadequate. They condone certain killing and allow more of it. They lack procedural due process for the fetus.

Interestingly enough, the supporters of the pro-abortion with no restrictions stance reject the reform legislation on essentially the same basis. They claim that any prohibitive laws whatever are unconstitutional since they ignore the issue of due process required under the Fourteenth Amendment. They maintain that reform laws only divert attention from the main injustice and discriminatory effect of such a restriction of freedom. Similarly, the proponents of abortion with no restrictions reject the reform laws as well on the ground that they do not afford equal protection to women, or procedural justice.

Thus, the inter-personal subjective orientation, which demands the judicious concern for special circumstances in the sense of human suffering and the quality of life, finds opposition from both the extreme pro-abortion position and the anti-abortion side. Of course, as indicated, their respective interpretations of impersonal objectivity differ according to the nature of the absolute value which they uphold.

Those who maintain the pro-abortion with regulation position argue that one who is faced with the abortion dilemma is caught between two absolute values: (1) the right of the fetus to life; (2) the right of the woman to self-determination. The controversy revolves around the question: Which rights take priority? The anti-abortionists typically insist that the absolute right to life must take precedence over other rights. Logically, without life the other rights are senseless to discuss. The proponents of the abortion with no restrictions, however, answer that potential life or life for the sake of mere existence does not qualify under the definition of "rights".

The controversy here, obviously, eminates from the classic distinction between acts performed by individuals that cause harm to others (public acts) and those that do not (private acts) (Mill, 1977). While the state may use its power to coerce the performance of (some) public acts, its control over private acts becomes an intrusion, so the classic argument goes, on personal liberty. Although abortion ostensibly fits into the category of interpersonal injury, since the fetus does not possess the capacity to be injured, abortion, so argue the pro-abortionits, belongs to the private realm.

In any case, the supporters of pro-abortion with regulation contend that by stating the problem in absolute terms we are always faced with the question of rank. This creates a stalemate condition. Callahan (1970) remarks that both extreme sides may be called "one-dimensional". If many of the issues regarding the ranking of rights were not stated in such absolute terms, their differences would be less accentuated. Callahan, therefore, presses for their expression in the context of the surrounding issues. He makes the following statement summarizing his position:

It is very rare for laws to be changed solely out of a concern for procedural questions of freedom and due process. They are usually changed because of a shift in the thinking or the attitude of the public toward the substantive issues at stake (409).

It is on the latter basis, that Callahan supports reform of the restrictive legal codes. Of the three guidelines proposed by

113

Callahan, two are especially pertinent. (The third is considered under another conceptual dimensions) He suggests -

(1) Morally, there are no automatic 'indications' for abortion; each case has to be judged individually, taking account of all circumstances;

(2) There are no automatic moral lines to be drawn against abortion; again each case must be judged individually... (18-19).

Callahan's main concern, which is characteristic of this basic position, is to develop a policy in which the moral or legal issues on abortion may be judiciously formulated. Generally, those in favor of the pro-abortion with regulations position ascribe to an inter-personal subjectivity orientation.

In summary, the anti-abortion stance depends on impersonal objectivity (i.e., the unqualified protection of the fetus) for the formulation of justice. For the opponents of abortion, even revised or less restrictive laws are unjust. Modification with reference to special circumstances merely serves to undermine the fundamental issue of the absolute right of life. Less restrictive laws essentially condone certain killing and allow more of it. (Irrespective of any special circumstances, e.g., poverty, deformity, rape, etc., abortion is not permissable since it is tantamount to killing for the sake of inconvenience.) Less restrictive laws lack procedural due process for the fetus since they undermine the absolute right to life.

Those in favor of repeal argue that any prohibitive laws whatever are unconsitutional since they do not afford procedural due process for the woman.

The supporters of pro-abortion with regulation, however, contend that stating the problem in absolute terms raises the question of rank and poses a stalemate. The reform position rests on inter-personal subjectivity -- judging each case individually, weighing all the special circumstances, including human suffering and the quality of life (i.e., the goal is substantive justice).

Improvement versus Stability

Social change raises innumerable awkward and intransigent issues in any theory of justice. The threshold of the problem is the intractable incongruity between the experience of justice in society and the unrelenting reality of social change. The concept of justice demands the specification of the goals of social change. Two recurring themes of change are found in the literature on justice: improvement and stability. The pair suggests the dilemma between benefiting from the demands of impulse and the immediate attention to social needs versus benefiting from general restraint and discipline.

In the first instance, justice depends on the occasion of opportunity and spontaneity to bring about some sort of social improvement. The connotation of spontaneity is in the natural and best sense of activity and self-control. Human progress is at the apex of concerns, including the extension of individual rational control over social life, technological advancement and a general alleviation of conflict in human life. Justice embraces the human capacity for reason and humanitarianism.

Theories of justice stressing stability usually present a less optimistic view of humankind. They point to the enormous cruelties and irrationalities evidenced in political and social history. With the possibility that advanced knowledge can be used as easily for destruction as for improvement of humankind, every accomplishment in the name of progress denotes an occasion for an even greater atrocity. The thrust of this orientation is not to protect the individual from the arbitrary interference of the state. Rather, emphasis is on safeguarding a particular social order from any temporary digression or some transitory demands. Confidence is placed on those forms of resolutions that have been developed and approved by history and on the capacity to move forward using a selective historical intelligence.

The dimension of Improvement versus Stability focuses on the effects or consequences of a specific proposal of justice. Essentially, what is involved here is the question of values: Do we, upon deciding on a just situation, seek to change society for the purpose of improving it; or do we seek to establish consistency over time for the purpose of preserving peace and tradition or the survival of the social order?

The prohibition of abortion is justified on the basis of stability. The anti-abortionists fear that relaxation or abolishment of strict abortion laws actually threatens the fundamental public peace. The general feeling is that the efforts to liberalize or repeal abortion laws merely represent a temporary digression from the social order. The implication being, that by altering the restrictive codes, the authorities are simply conceding to a transitory popular demand. Noonan (1970) epitomizes this position:

Law prohibiting abortion had taught a view of life and responsibility, and the law cannot be abolished without substantial impact on the moral consciousness of Americans (xi).

Affirming this stance, Ralph Potter (1969) writes that "abortion is a symbolic threat to an entire system of thought and meaning" (101). He suggests that even when we are successful in arguing, that it is "not an actual threat to minimal public order, it is nevertheless, a symbolic threat to the moral order espoused by Christians for two millennia" (101).

Many anti-abortionists contend that prohibitive laws embody the Judeo-Christian tradition against the destruction of innocent human life (e.g., Thomas O'Donnell, 1970). There are others (e.g., St. John-Stevas, 1964), who argue that the concept of the right to life is at the root of the Western tradition of rationality, and is accepted by many who would reject Christian-Judiaic doctrine. In an effort to make the case for the latter, David Louisell and John Noonan (1970) attempt to demonstrate a precedence for the non-violability of the human life in English and American law. They claim that there is a distinct tradition of movement in the law to protect the fetus throughout its existence within the womb (226).

The prohibitionist's emphasis on stability and on the maintainance of the status quo also has symbolic overtones for the family as the building block of society. The general contention is that wide acceptance of abortion may result in an ultimate decline of the "mother-role" in society, and may even weaken the family unit as the fundamental institution of society. (e.g., Greer and Keating, 1978)

The changes that reform or repeal embody often pose a very real threat to certain minority groups. Since poor blacks and other minority groups are the largest potential users of abortion (Hall, 1965), the pro-abortion movement is sometimes construed as a subtle attempt at a systematic dissolution of certain minorities and the poor (Williams, 1978). This reconstruction is real especially when we note the types of plans advocated by some population alarmists, which includes extensive and forced contraception, and abortion only with sterilization as a "package deal" (See Combs & Welch, 1982; Williams, 1981).

For whatever reason, most anti-abortionists agree that any changes of the prohibitive laws governing abortion under the guise of improvement are unwarranted. Reform or repeal is seen to be threatening to the public peace and established tradition. They argue that any justification on the basis of reform or improvement will prove to be transitory and relative at best.

Both pro-abortion positions justify their stance in terms of improvement. Reform or repeal, whatever the case may be, is assumed to solve many social and individual problems. Therefore, reform or repeal constitutes an improvement over the old restrictive system. In order to make their case for improvement both sides usually consider the detrimental aspects of forcing repressive laws upon the individual or the society. For example, they often emphasize the illegal organization which may be characteristic of a strict system. Or, they may point to the relative inefficiency of the anti-abortion laws by quoting the maternal death rate, illegitimate birth rates, and the incredible cost to taxpayers. The underlying assumption is, of course, that the reform or repeal will effect an improvement over these conditions.

The pro-abortion rebuttle to the anti-abortion claims usually takes the form of disputing the legal continuity of the restrictive codes. The notion that the prohibitions are necessary for public order is rejected. Even if it were the original intent of the law to protect the fetus, the vast number of evasions of the law demonstrates the inability of the law to effectively protect the prenatal life. But more importantly, it is argued that the original intent of the law is not designed to protect the fetus. Rather, it is intends to protect the woman from a dangerous and often fatal surgical procedure (Means, 1971). Cyril Means refers to this as the "relative safety test". She suggests that the law usually demands the "least dangerous alternative."

Accordingly, it is argued, that in light of the development of more sophisticated medical techniques, the anti-abortion laws are antiquated. They need reform or repeal. Indeed, apart from, perhaps, reinforcing the idea of keeping women in their inferior place, the repressive codes miss their mark.

Alleviating the degree of human suffering indicated in the estimated prevelance of illegal abortions and the adverse effects on the family, the mother, and the child who are victimized by an unwanted birth provide the general context of the justification of abortion, in the sense of improvement. The proponents of either reform or repeal both insist that the general expression of the public's willingness to reconsider the prohibitive laws of abortion demonstrates some indication that a growing number of individuals do not regard abortion in purely the traditional sense.

The concept of justice ultimately provides a view of the world. It describes the relationship between the individual and society.

Justice based on other consciousness assumes the voluntary subordination of private values to the values of the community or society. It does not imply the exclusion of individual interests. Societal interests are believed to derive their legitimacy through individual acceptance.

A judgment of justice depends on the outcome or the attending affects on the whole community or society. Appraising actions in terms of social consequences may be viewed from two perspectives: First, an action or decision may be judged "just" if it yields social order or public peace. Second, an action or a decision may be judged "just" if it results in the common good or general well-being of individuals in society.

Justice conceived in reference to inner consciousness negates the notion that a judgment can be made on the basis of externalities such as security or some collective interests. Justice must go beyond the beneficial results of the governing principles. It must penetrate the inner character and motives of the individuals. The individual is assumed to be rational, responsible and socially acute.

Two questions evolve: First, on what ground can one justify any social curbs imposed upon human liberty, as in the social demand to subordinate certain individual rights to the welfare of other individuals? Second, on what basis can one justify the maximum freedom of individuals to pursue certain personal interests, or the non-control of human behavior?

The abortion controversy demonstrates heavy reliance on the emotive power and symbolic implications of the social versus the individual points of reference. That the abortion dilemma is laden with emotional overtones may be evidenced by the dependence on pictures representing the mutilated fetus; or such symbols as a coffin representing the dead mother; or the description of nightmares as Nazism, illustrating certain extreme ramifications of brute force.

The main point of maintaining or passing prohibitive abortion laws is to assure and reinforce an "other" consciousness. It is generally argued that an "other" consciousness underlies the fundamental peace and well-being of

118

the community or society. David Granfield (1969) aptly poses the question for most anti-abortionists when he writes:

> Whether our ethical convictions are that "the direct killing of an unborn child is always immoral," or that "every woman has the right to abort a child she does not want," we are faced here with a political question which transcends the individual case: How do these permitted killings or the prohibition of them affect the common good? (148)

It is frequently argued that the only efficient way to insure the survival of humankind is by placing the other-consciousness over and above any personal motives to destroy human life for reasons of inconvenience. Catering to the personal necessity of seeking abortion is often construed as representing an indifference to the value of a human life. John Finnis (1970) expresses this idea in the following:

> The criminal law, with the penal process, is the symbolic drama by which the socially preferred range of values is vindicated against indifference and affront (179).

Ralph Potter (1969) discusses the Christian concern for preserving the "other" consciousness:

> The willingness to practice abortion, or even to condone resort to abortion by others, signals that the high Christian vision of selfless charity has become despised and rejected by men. The Christian portrayal of the true man as one characterized by selflessness, sacrifice, concern for the weak and the unlovely, and a willingness to accept and transcend allotted afflictions through the power of redemptive suffering has faded in public consciousness to the point that it can seldom induce willing imitation (25).

Other-consciousness is thought to underlie harmony in society. The concept is rudimentary to the Christian notion of social order. The internalization of an "other" consciousness, or in the Christian version, selflessness, is not just the product of any common morality of a certain time or culture. Both the secular and the religious advocates of the anti-abortion position would probably agree that when a mother chooses self-sacrifice it is out of a deep internalization of an "other" consciousness. No specific instance of social pressure could even enforce this. Following this line of argument, abortion prohibitions are intended to inculcate a special view of life which safeguards the human life from ultimate demise. It insures social solidarity.

119

Noonan (1970) describes the legal function, when he says that, "the public teaching embodied in the law tells the uncertain man - and on many matters we are all uncertain men - what is right to do" (xi). In the moment of decision, by complying with the abortion laws, one necessarily sacrifices some amount of personal freedom and thereby demonstrates an "other" consciousness and agreement over the social value of human life.

"Other" consciousness is also a major component of the justification of the pro-abortion with regulation stance. The interpretation is slightly different from the one characterizing the anti-abortion perspective. The meaning of "other" consciousness is usually considered in the sense of empathy or "verstehen" for the human condition. There are two aspects to the "other" consciousness element in the pro-abortion-with regulation position. In the first instance, references to "other" consciousness is found in the justification of the permissibility of abortions. In the second instance, the "other" consciousness is suggested in the justification of some sort of regulation over the medical procedure of abortion.

The arguments, in the former sense, often attempt to appeal to a social sensitivity or "verstehen" of the detrimental consequences suffered by society when a significant minority is coerced by law. Their argument has lost some of its impact since passage of the 1977 Hyde Amendment curtailing Medicaid payments for abortions. One of the major arguments against this amendment was that it would discriminate against the poor who relied on federal funds for abortions. Despite hostile debates in Congress, and a compromise (abortions where permitted when the mother's life was endangered) the Hyde Amendment passed the House with a vote of 256 to 114 and the Senate with a vote of 47 to 21 (Vinovskis, 1980).

Common acceptance of some social good is necessary to legitimate social prohibitions. It is argued that when a substantial portion of society rejects the claim that a particular social restriction is for the common good, a re-evaluation is in order. Rephrased, this means that, when popular support for certain laws diminishes, as in the case of abortion, the indication may be that the extent of the common ground on which the community or society is organized has been over-stepped. It no longer functions in the social interest. Its demands, in the sense of "other" consciousness, may be inappropriate.

The individual tragedies and social injustices which make life so unbearable also make the decision of abortion very difficult. The amount of human suffering or the social indignation experienced by both mother and child in such cases as rape and incest, or abnormality usually provides the subject matter in the justification of reform. But a justification focusing on a single individual is a relatively rare occurrence in the pro-abortion-with regulation position. (The reference groups usually consist of the poor, unwed mothers, deformed children, unwanted children, family, doctors, community or society, etc.) In both the anti-abortion or pro-abortion with regulation there is some sort of reference group which is the object of the projected detrimental consequences. The benefit of the "other" constitutes the justification of the particular stand on the abortion dilemma. In the reform position, the reference group consists of the society of women, the medical professionals, the family, the unwanted children, or the community or society at large.

Taking for instance the case of unwanted children, Hans Forssman and Inga Thuwe in "One Hundred and Twenty Children Born After the Application for Therapeutic Abortion Refused," (1971) report the following: (1) Unwanted children are more likely to require psychiatric consultation and hospitalization (probability = .05). (2) The names of unwanted children are more likely to be listed on the registration for delinquency at the children's aid bureaus (p = .05). (3) Unwanted children are in need more often for public assistance between the ages of 16 and 25, than the control groups (p = .01). (4) Unwanted children get a significantly lesser amount of education than the control subjects. (5) They are more often exempted from military service. (6) The family environment of the unwanted children suggests that, generally, they have <u>not</u> had the advantage of a secure childhood life.

Forssman and Thuwe conclude that:

...the very fact a woman applies for legal abortion means that the prospective child runs a risk of having to surmount greater social and mental handicaps than its peers, even when the grounds for the application are so slight that it is refused (143).

In the United States "tens of thousands of children [are] severely battered or killed" (Reiterman, 1971: 68). One may ask as Mildred Beck (1971) does:

How many of the abusive parents had given clues that the pregnancy was unwanted? (69)

Advocates of the pro-abortion with regulation position generally contend, that regardless of what individual moralities dictate, we simply cannot objectively prove that abortion constitutes a threat to the common good. On the contrary, it is usually on behalf of the common good that reform is sought. From this point of view, society does not have a legitimate right to block an abortion which a woman may be seeking, except in very special instances. Accordingly, limitation of action can only be considered in situations which represent a danger to the common good. Regulation, then, is justified on the primary assumption of social interest.

The regulations may include the specification of time limits when abortions are permissible. After a certain period of time in the pregnancy abortion may not be allowed except to save the life of the mother. The regulatory scheme may also include the specification of acceptable surgical procedures and facilities, or the licensing of abortionists. Different authors, of course, recommend different types of regulations; but they all usually justify them in terms of some sort of reference group, as the community or society. Rarely are the recommendations justified in terms of a singular individual right.

More often than not, it is the maximization of rights in a pluralistic society, which is the prevaling theme in the justification of the pro-abortion with regulation position. Callahan (1970), for example, argues that to acknowledge only an inner consciousness perspective, as the woman's right to control her own body responsibly, would imply that the woman is beyond the normal limitation of human community existence. The individual right of a woman to be treated without discrimination or without male domination is distinct from being absolved of the obligation to regard the rights of others. Callahan admits that it is probable that most advocates of the inner consciousness perspective are not really referring to the extreme implications. But, then, he claims, they never make the effort to specify the limitations (409).

What Callahan suggests, is that, perhaps, much of the conflict over rights would appear far less problematic, if an other consciousness perspective, and the idea of a maximization of rights, were the aim of justice. In certain respects the pro-abortion with regulation position represents an interesting compromise between the extreme restrictive and non-restrictive perspectives. It must be noted, however, that both extreme positions usually agree that legalizing abortion with certain restrictions provides an unsatisfactory solution. The anti-abortionists insist on their own interpretation of "other" consciousness. Brody (1975) retorts by saying:

> In an age where we doubt the justice of capital punishment even for very dangerous criminals, killing a fetus who has not done any harm, to avoid a future problem it may pose, seems totally unjust.

There are indeed many social problems that could be erased simply by destroying those persons who constitute or cause them, but what is a solution repugnant to the values of society itself (36-37).

The supporters of pro-abortion with no restrictions, however, emphasize the inner consciousness dimension in their justification of claims. Alice Rossi speaks for many who ascribe to the pro-abortion with no restrictions position when she states:

> The passage of ... a reform statute is only one step on the way to the goal of maximum individual freedom for men and women to control their own reproductive lives. Such freedom should include the personal right to undo a contraceptive failure by means of a therapeutic abortion .... The only criterion should be whether such an induced abortion is consistent with the individual woman's personal set of moral and religious values,and that is something only she can judge (Callahan, 1971:461).

Thus, the justification favoring abortion without restrictions stems from the idea that the woman must be the sole controller of her body, and as such, only she can decide whether to bear children or not. The general contention is that an individual's personal freedom may only be restrained by the legitimate rights of other individuals in society. The position does not admit the legitimacy of any other claims or rights in the case of abortion. To be master of one's own body is considered to be an inalienable right (Weddington, 1982: 17).

Maurine Neuberger (1971) implies that appeals for "other" consciousness are all too often merely reduced to men's interests. She writes:

> In conclusion, I reflect on my long activity in behalf of the status of women. Men make the laws. Do they still believe that women are their chattels? Do they subconsciously feel that women are not virtuous?

> Who decides when life begins? Men, who have never borne nor suckled a child. Who drew up the laws declaring that a woman has no control over the use of her own body? The inseminators. Who sees that these laws are sustained? Men. For what reasons? In their terms: for the sake of the soul, for the preservation of the family, for the good of society, the economy, the state, the wars of conquest. But

whose society? Whose markets? Whose state? Whose wars? Certainly not women's (113).

The general presumption is that no interest of society can be objectively placed over or above the right of individual's to control their bodies. Garrett Hardin (1967) asserts that the only way women will be free "from a now needless form of slavery" or will be the "masters" of their bodies is to "emancipate" women from the "pregnancies they do not want" (82).

In a summary of the 1973 Roe versus Wade decision, Sarvis and Rodman (1974) conclude that:

> Of the four major constitutional issues that were being debated between 1969-1972 - the woman's privacy, equal protection, vagueness, and the rights of the fetus - the court's decision hinged upon the first (64).

As in most discussions of the right to privacy, the court conceded that "the constitution does not explicitly mention any [such] right" (410 U.S. at 152). However, a long line of cases has recognized through several amendments "a guarantee of certain areas or zones of privacy" and "makes it clear that the right has some extension to activities relating to "marriage, procreation, contraception, family relations, child rearing and education" (410 U.S. at 152-53). Based on this rather tenuous phrasing, e.g., "has some extension to," the court declared "This right of privacy...is broad enough to encompass a woman's decision whether or not to terminate her pregnancy" (410 U.S. at 153). The opinion, according to many, leaves ambiguous whether the court actually affirmed the "unlimited right to do with one's body as one pleases" (410 U.S. at 154).[12]

Despite the broadness of the interpretation of "right to privacy", the court concluded that the intervention by the state in the abortion decision is indeed unconstituional. As we have previously noted, this decision was expanded and reaffirmed in the June 15, 1983 decision.

Given these changes, then, abortion is viewed as an individual problem and requires only an inner consciousness. Alice Rossi affirms this position when she writes:

> The only criterion should be whether such an induced abortion is consistent with the individual woman's personal set of moral and religious values, and that is something only she can judge (Callahan, 1971:461).

124

Perfectionism versus Practicality

Should justice be expressed with reference to ideals or facts? Perfectionism refers to a position where humanity is moving toward a greater awareness and realization of ideal justice. The practicality perspective confines justice to immediate experience or facts.

The perfectionist orientation suggests that human beings are in a perpetual pursuit of the knowledge of universal justice, i.e., the harmonious fulfillment of the human personality in society. The persistence of the search for social justice implies that there is a perfect justice. The notion of perfect justice assumes that human beings, when given the opportunity, will strive by the most enlightened method at their disposal to establish maximum social justice (i.e., the idea that science is ultimately used for the benefit of human beings). Scientific progress of the movement, which, ever since the Middle Ages, has been increasing in momentum, finds its logical climax in the perfectionism of the individual and the realization of justice in some universal sense.

The expanding approximation of a universal reality is already partially expressed in every individual. When all the involved parties to a conflict over justice can agree on a reasonable and just resolution, a certain portion of the rational system of ideal justice is exposed by finite reason. (Sociologically, this implies a doctrine of symbolic relationships. The nature of social knowledge depends on the incidence of human relationships. Social knowledge cannot be fully grasped until these relationships are at least symbolically exhausted.)

Theories which posit a perfect justice exert a great deal of energy deriving universal standards of behavior defending some supreme good. Little attention is given to practical import. Many theories are associated with some utopian vision.

In contrast, theories underscoring practicality usually repudiate anything ideal or final, whether in human nature or society. Emphasis is on a precise methodology for understanding social problems. Justice from a practicality perspective stays very close to the social facts and commonly attempts to inspire policy and decision-making. It leads to an exclusive emphasis on the practical and the immediately verifiable elements in life, as distinguished from the remote substance of idealism or utopianism of the perfectionist perspective. There is a tendency to translate the meaning of justice in terms of doing or undoing, resulting in the reconstruction of mental experiences and in the mental adaptation of certain social facts.

Much of the anti-abortion position is permeated by a religious framework, especially, in the discussion of the value of human life. The argument, typically revolving around the valuation of fetal life, is aimed at convincing one that abortion is a sin or morally wrong. The position, therefore, points to the possibility of a sinless world. To this extent, it imputes the quality of perfectionism. However, this sequence of ideas does not form the pivotal point of the anti-abortionist contribution to the abortion controversy. The crux of the problem lies in the justification of the imposition of the legal prohibition of abortion to all of the members of society.

The justification of a restrictive legal code, however, is generally considered in pragmatic terms. The problem becomes one of finding the most effective way to safeguard the value of the inviolability of human life. To both the religious and secular supporters of anti-abortion, strict prohibitions against abortion comprise the most practical and the most efficient method to suppress abortions in all but rare cases. Sarvis and Rodman (1974) report that:

> Anti-abortionists used to play down the number of criminal abortions (giving low estimates of 10,000 to 200,000 per year) while pro-abortion dramatised the amount of harm done to many who had criminal abortions (giving high estimates of 200,000 to 1.5 million per year) (26).

The anti-abortionists argue that despite the number of estimated illegal abortions, there are far less abortions performed when the legal codes are strict. They often try to prove by using international data, that with legalization of abortion, there is a vast increase of abortions. For example, there are cases where the legalization of abortion resulted in such a dramatic decline in birth rate that the laws were reversed.

Moreover, the anti-abortionists try to demonstrate, by referring to the international experience, that legalized abortion does <u>not</u> necessarily mean that a decrease in the amount of underground or unethical abortions will follow. For instance, Fred Mecklenburg (1972) writes:

> It is widely believed that legalizing abortion will eliminate the problems of criminal abortion. This, however, is verifiably untrue ... (Accumulated data is worldwide, including reference from the German Democratic Republic, Japan, Great Britain, Yugoslavia. Hungary, Czechoslavakia, Bulgaria, Poland, USSR and Canada) (50).

There is also the anti-utopian argument, with visions of Nazism, implying that voluntary abortion may evolve into involuntary abortion, and open the way to compulsory sterilization. Those who are concerned over Black genocide often employ this line of argumentation. Some of the past bills which have been introduced in various state legislatures have demanded that mothers of illegitimate children submit to sterilization, or suffer jail sentences, or lose certain welfare benefits (Paul, 1968).

Finally, the justification of a law against abortion usually does not focus on any perfectionist or idealistic tendency of humankind. Rather, the individual is depicted as weak or vulnerable. The purpose of the law is to guide and to indicate what is right. Accordingly, Noonan (1970) claims:

A fuller view of the functions of law understands that the law channels action and, channelling shapes conduct and inculcates attitudes (xi).

Thus, the anti-abortion advocates agree that prohibitive abortion laws are, in a practical sense, necessary to protect human procreation. They assure a minimum moral standard of the inviolability of human life in society.

The pro-abortion with regulation position also aspires to a practical type of justification. The interpretation of this differs slightly from the one considered by the anti-abortionists. The advocates of pro-abortion with regulation usually emphasize the impracticality and detrimental aspects of forcing restrictive laws upon the public, and they attempt to make the case for the practicality of allowing abortions and regulating the conditions.

The advocates of pro-abortion with regulation point to the differential opportunity of various social groups to choose legitimate alternatives in a restrictive jurisdiction. Socio-economic and marital status are important differentiating factors. It is noted that prior to reform the ratio of abortions to live births in private hospitals were far greater than in public (non-profit) hospitals or clinics. In restrictive jurisdictions affluent women have a greater chance of finding a compliant practitioner, or have a greater opportunity to travel to another area, where the laws are less prohibitive. In addition, unmarried women in restrictive areas usually have less opportunity than married women to obtain therapeutic abortions or finding compliant practitioners (Schur, 1965).

The alternatives for most women in prohibitive jurisdictions, it is argued, are less than satisfactory. The woman may have to carry the fetus to term, and, perhaps, give it an unsatisfactory or substandard home life. They run the risk of obtaining an abortion by an incompetent and often expensive service. She may attempt a self-induced abortion, or consent to an unwanted sterilization. This limited set of alternatives poses the abnormally high statistical probability of rather severe social consequences. Hence, from a practical standpoint the prohibitions against abortion must be reconsidered.

There is also the argument that legislation must conform to the reality of the situation or the time. The general allegation is that restrictive abortion laws are unrealistic and unworkable. This reason alone requires reform. But, regardless of the exact contents of the arguments propounded by the pro-abortion with regulation side, they all seem to demonstrate a common preoccupation with ready identification, immediacy, and practicality.

The supporters of pro-abortion without restrictions are unique on this dimension. They generally lean toward a perfectionist explanation. Lawrence Lader (1966), for example, suggests that if personal choice and ultimate responsibility over the "positive control" of reproduction were informally reinforced, the "century of the wanted child" would be within the realm of possibility. In the words of Lader:

> [By not passing] legislation allowing individual conscience and free choice in abortion, the core of our democratic system is crippled. The right to abortion is the foundation of society's long struggle to guarantee that every child comes into this world wanted, loved, and cared for. The right to abortion along with all birth-control measures, must establish the century of the wanted child (166).

The pro-abortion with no restrictions advocates often emphasize the most positive features of humankind. They generally try to assure their opponents that people, when given maximum freedom over their lives, will act responsibly. Further, it is believed that when given the choice, people will use science and technology to build a more perfect society or world.

In speculating about the reasons why the pro-abortionist's position has recently found more appeal than the anti-abortionist's side, Sarvis and Rodman (1974) comment on the growing momentum of a secularized brand of idealism:

> The pro-abortion argument also provides reassurance that people can and will use technology to create a better world. In a complex society filled with remote and uncontrollable forces, the promise of total and individual control over an

128

important part of life appeals to many. Most are aware of the awesome power of science and technology to bring about destruction and of the individual's limited control over these forces. People want and need to be reassured that technology will create a better world for them; they do not want to be presented with a vision of a Nazi state that uses technology to enforce its will. Given the growing prominence of a scientific and secular world view, a changing set of secular standards, and an increasingly recognized need for family planning, it is of little wonder if a vision of the century of the wanted child wins out over a vision of a Nazi state (25).

Sanctioned Duty versus Private Duty

The relationship between the concept of justice and the element of obligation is also among the essential themes covered by the writing on justice. The literature generally deals with this problem insofar as we may distinguish between the external character of sanctioned duty and the internal character of private duty.

Sanctioned duty refers to the authoritative nature of laws and norms and the subtle obligatory force derived from them. The obligatory element in justice is determined by the pattern of laws or the normative social order. The range of expectations for social behavior is limited and clearly defined. Sanctioned duty and morality are fused in the social order and instituted by the state. Moreover, only these formal norms can provide an objective and determinate criteria for justice. Justice is established and reinforced by the objective order in society.

Theories depending on private duty encompass a broad and undefined range of expectations, drawing upon an inward obligation of one's own conscience and spontaneity of thought. In any given situation one may feel a certain sense of duty which goes far beyond any legal prescription. Obligation originates within the individual and from the principle on which the action or decision is motivated.

Private duty refers to the implied duty rising out of an individual conscience or an inner sense of social responsibility, and a self-commitment to behave humanely. This latter notion of duty tends to encompass the whole human personality. Not every social interaction has a precise legal meaning or is included in some legal definition. All human interactions impute

129

some moral implications with none beyond the realm of moral connotation.

Justice in this sense is tied to the notions of rectitude and love. The individual responsibility to uphold human dignity suggests that the motivation to act justly is without any extraneous pressure or influence. Weight is given to the subjective sense of what is right and what is necessary to do.

Since an attitude against abortion is usually accompanied by the demand for laws to prohibit the action, the focus is necessarily on sanctioned duty. Sanctions against abortion are meant to indicate a clear preference for the value of human life. Laws morally guide the weak and unsure and they establish the societal moral foundation which provides a pattern for acceptable behavior. It is feared that with lifting the abortion prohibitions, the state will be viewed as reinforcing the objectification of human life.

The supporters of this general perspective hold that individual morality can be reduced to many relative abstractions about what is right or wrong, which are impossible to reconcile. It is argued that reliance on individual morality may be misleading or even harmful to human welfare. The inviolability of human life, however, is considered not to be an abstraction, but a fundamental principle of civilization. Sanctions against abortion indicate a clear preference for the value of human life. Sanctions serve the purpose of the implementation of a social policy which clearly rejects other competing systems of values. Granfield (1969), writes that, "Law has a dual function: It points the finger and it makes a fist" (175).

It is popularly thought, that in the midst of competing moralities, the individual often becomes confused about the right thing to do. Moreover, it is alleged that most people have a need for the distinct specification of acceptable behavior and the clarification of human goals. Heavy sanctions or restrictive laws are seen as unnecessary. They morally guide the weak and the unsure, and they establish the societal moral standard which can be used to pattern behavior.

There is another side of the anti-abortionist point of view, which is distinctly humanistic, in the affirmation of society's rights to sanction "the inviolability of life." Granfield (1969), in his discussion of "absurdity and abortion", makes the case for humanism as follows:

> For Camus, absurdity refers to the conflict between man's inquiring mind and the silence of the universe. Man has nostalgia for unity in a fragmented world.

. . . .

By setting up this fundamental affirmation - "the right of others to life" - Camus hit at the heart of nihilism, which reduces men to expendable units of social utility.

. . . .

In passionate reaction, Camus forged a philosophic defense of all human life. He isolated that ideological disease which has so infected modern civilization - the objectification of man (127-129).

We can infer from the passage that, "This objectification is at the root of the problem of liberal abortion" (129). Similarly, Brody (1975) argues, that one of the major disadvantages to no abortion laws is that their elimination has a greater probability of being understood by the public as evidence that "the state condone(s) all abortions, and not as maintenance by the state of a standard of neutrality on the issue of abortion" (61). It is feared that with the lifting of the abortion prohibitions, the state will be viewed as reinforcing the "objectification" of human life.

Although the reform advocates insist on some sort of regulations, the final decision is left to the woman and her physician. Non-restrictive laws allow the maximization of rights including the rights of the various individuals to pursue their own moralities, and the right of doctors to provide the best health care possible without state interference.

According to the repeal position the obligation to act responsibly must flow from one's own moral dictates. One is ultimately accountable to oneself. Proscribing abortion does not secure or promote individual morality, nor does liberalizing abortion work to enervate the Christian ethic or tend to encourage promiscuity. The fundamental challenge to the restrictive legal code is that it constitutes an invasion of the personal freedom of the woman.

Although private duty is an inherent element in the justification of the repeal and reform positions, each presents us with a distinct interpretation.

Callahan (1970) represents the reform position when he writes:

. . . While abortion laws ought not to be repealed, they should be free enough to place the final decision in the hands of the pregnant woman (19).

It is generally claimed that irrespective of any laws prescribing abortion, the woman and the doctor in the final analysis, are still left with their consciences to decide whether they are morally right or wrong. They are left ultimately with their social and religious convictions to reconcile this final decision; the contention is that respect for life cannot be entirely dictated by the letter of the law. It must, essentially, emanate from the individual conscience. In addition, it is denied that permission of abortion or the decision to abort constitutes a fundamental disrespect for human life.

For many, the rationalization for extending the right to abortion derives from an appreciation of the problem of freedom in a pluralistic society, with many divergent viewpoints at play. Callahan writes that:

> the strength of pluralistic societies lies in the personal freedom they afford individuals (493).

Again, non-restrictive laws are designed to allow the maximum expression of rights. The rights of the mother, family, doctor, and society are all considered. Justice, from this perspective, appeals to extending the right to various minorities to pursue their own moralities. Private duty, rather than sanctioned duty, is at the core of a just resolution in this sense.

The point is often made that quality health care is also a right, which cannot be circumscribed by law. The basic issue of the right of doctors to make medical judgments without interference from the state is accompanied by the question of the right to designate or limit the extent of duty to provide quality health care to patients. The medical professional ethic, especially, must depend on the private moral duty to help humankind. Again, irrespective of any abortion laws or professional codes, the doctor, in the final analysis, must account for his/her own personal decision. Thus, the doctor must not be legally held to provide or deny abortions, and must be left to his/her moral responsibility to provide the best health care possible.

As stated above, the pro-abortion with no restrictions position also ascribes to private duty; however, there is a slightly different accent. For example, the Committee for the Advancement of Psychiatry in the book, The Right to Abortion (1970) concludes that:

> . . . 'For those who take this moral stand (that abortion constitutes murder) there perhaps can be no absolute rebuttal, and certainly those who take this position will themselves avoid abortion and will be shocked by those who condone it.' But it is

132

also true that such people do not need the law to support their moral principles (GAP, 1970: 11).

After three years of study and debate the committee recommended that:

> . . . abortion, when performed by a licensed physician be entirely removed from the domain of criminal law. We believe that a woman should have the right to abort or not just as she has the right to marry or not (12).

The American Civil Liberties Union also affirms that all "criminal sanctions should be removed from the area of abortion . . ." The "laws and standards governing this medical procedure should be the same as those which govern the performance of all medical procedures" (GAP, 1970: 27).

Regardless of the exact shape of the argument or the nature of the rights which may be violated by a restrictive legal code, the fundamental challenge to it stems from its invasion of the personal freedom of the woman. Social control through law is considered to be destructive of justice. It is deemed at odds with the democratic values. That humans should propagate their kind is a natural enough phenomenon. This should be a comparatively remote concern of justice. The valued significance of humankind is unavoidable. Any sanctioning of the same is unwarranted.

The slogan: "one cannot legislate morality" is particularly appropriate in this specific context. Prescribing abortion does not promote or secure individual morality, nor does liberalizing abortion work to enervate the Christian ethics or tend to encourage promiscuity.

Garrett Hardin (1967) asserts that the legal prohibition against abortion is tantamount to a forced pregnancy. While forced behavior resulting from law is not uncommon in organized social life, Hardin stipulates that it may become offensive if it questions the individual conscience. If it, at the same time, may be proved that no substantive harm would be incurred with their removal the prohibition becomes even more offensive. Hardin submits that the prohibitions essentially undermine individual integrity by limiting the freedom of choice, and are justifiably objectionable on this basis (69-86).

C. Comment, Summary, and Future Implications of the Conceptual Model

The conceptualization of justice necessiates making choices among competing values. It suggests a continuous crystalization of different types of values which regulate social interaction in times of conflict.

Conceptually, justice reflects certain patterns of values that people use as general guidelines for their own actions, for judging the actions of others and for indicating the direction of future actions. A decision of justice involves choice and the organization of values in human conduct. The conceptual dimensions attempt to capture the crucial elements of the decision-making process involved in the conceptualization of justice.

Each dilemma as expressed by the sets of conceptual dimensions has survived despite the subjective interpretation or treatment by many different theorists and irrespective of the historical and cultural contexts. It is the transformation or reinterpretation of certain persisting values which implies the degree to which constant elements of justice interact with social reality.

The abortion controversy suggests that the nature of justification reflects the underlying value systems which influence individual and group decisions. Since any justification of any position on abortion necessitates the selection of certain values or definitions among alternatives, it inevitably entails forsaking the attractive features of the rejected alternatives and accepting the negative features of the chosen alternative. Any position in the abortion controversy may simultaneously give rise to certain inherent sources of justice and of injustice.

The first position, which prohibits abortion in most cases except under rare conditions, seems intent upon the State's commitment to and confirmation of the "inviolability of human life." The position is justified on the grounds that it is necessary to protect human life from self-demise. The traditional Hobbesian problem of order is suggested by the model. It is not surprising, then, that the pattern of dimensions associated with the anti-abortion position resemble the Normative Conformity construct of justice (see Table Five). The conceptual dimensions linked with Normative Conformity justice include: sameness; impersonal objectivity; stability; other-consciousness; practicality; and sanctioned duty. Stability and sanctioned duty serve to differentiate the Normative Conformity construct of justice from the other two.

ANTI-ABORTION PATTERN OF ISSUES

The points of development are
equal and must all be given same
consideration.

Sameness . . . ■ . . . . Diversity

Absolute right to life argument
over any consideration for
special circumstances.

Inter-personal . . . . ■ . . Impersonal
subjectivity   objectivity

Precedence with English Common law
which protects fetal life - maintain
Christian-Judiaic tradition.

Improvement . . . . ■ . . Stability

Christian value of selflessness
and commitment to social order.

Other- . . . ■ . . . . Inner-
consciousness   consciousness

Law is most efficient way to
assure morality and order.

Perfectionism . . . . ■ . . Practicality

Everyone needs guidance. The
weak must be formally obligated
to uphold moral standards of
society.

Sanctioned Duty . . ■ . . . . Private Duty

Note: The pattern of issues resembles the Normative
Conformity construct of justice.

The anti-abortion literature corroborates a similar pattern of issues, relating to the justness of the abortion decision.

The anti-abortion position empahsizes sameness, as in equal treatment for the fetus (i.e., commutative justice). The advocates of the anti-abortion position try to demonstrate the essential similarities or the equality among the various stages of development. All stages of the life cycle as well as all stages of human development are considered equal and therefore warrant equal protection before the law.

According to this position, abortion cannot be justified for any reason. Emphasis on the generality of rules (procedural justice) for the protection of the "absolute right to life" expresses the impersonal objectivity dimension of justice.

Concentration on the preservation of the Christian-Judiaic ethic or precedence with the English Common Laws which prohibit abortion form an important element in the anti-abortion justification pattern. Establishing continuity with tradition or history is captured under the stability dimension.

The Christian-Judiaic value of selflessness is often emphasized in the arguments against abortion. In a broader sense, it is maintained that social order or peace is only possible through developing and sustaining an other-consciousness or selfless orientation. Accordingly, the orientation looks more to the consequences of behavior rather than the motives behind it.

Both the religious and secular supporters of the anti-abortion position affirm the practical role of the law in the abortion question. Legal prohibitions are believed to be the most effective way to keep down the total number of abortions. Laws are considered to be the main way to formally reinforce the traditional moral order. Therefore, law must, in the most practical sense, be connected with the anti-abortion position. The justification of anti-abortion laws rarely emphasizes human virtues or perfect human nature. Rather the individual is usually described as weak and vulnerable.

Since an attitude against abortion is usually accompanied by the demand for laws to prohibit the action, the focus is necessarily on sanctioned duty. Because abortion is wrong, the individuals who are weak of charcter need guidance. The weak must be made to uphold the moral tradition of society to protect human life. This is most effectively approached through law. The legal system serves to determine the minimal acceptable standard of behavior. It underlies the public order. One is, according to this line of argumentation, obligated to abide by it and enforce it.

The position which favors some sort of regulation of abortion, but not the prohibition of abortion, seems to rise out of a desire to mitigate conflict in a pluralistic society. It extends rights to as many as possible, i.e., the woman, the family, the doctor, the state. In other words, it attempts to make as many happy as possible. In this respect, the pro-abortion with regulation stance resembles the Public Interest construct of justice (see Table Six). Public Interest justice emphasizes the following conceptual pattern: diversity; inter-personal subjectivity; improvement; other-consciousness; practicality; and private duty. The two identifying dimensions of this construct are diversity and inter-personal subjectivity. The pro-abortion with regulation position and Public Interest justice are comparable.

The regulatory aspect of this position is not designed to prohibit abortions. Characteristically, the policies merely suggest various ways to regulate abortions, e.g., by prescribing the conditions under which the operation may take place. Justification of pro-abortion with regulation is usually derived from an appreciation of the diversity between the various life-cycle stages. It is argued, that each stage of human development deserves special consideration. While the fetus is not on equal level with the human being, it is not merely a piece of body tissue to be indiscriminately disposed of either.

Further, not only must one consider the unique features of the different stages of life; the position also appeals to a consideration of the special and related circumstances (inter-personal subjectivity) which may be involved in the decision-making process. The system of justice must be flexible enough to accommodate the specific problems which comprise the question of justice.

It is also suggested that advanced medical technology and new knowledge warrant a change of the traditional attitudes and methods of handling the abortion dilemma. In order to meet the public demand for a better quality of life and good health care, it is necessary to allow abortions, and to regulate the conditions. Meeting individual needs and extending rights to various interests, according to this position, are associated with the movement to improve society.

The maximization of rights in society, however, implies some limitation to individual autonomy. This is justified in terms of an "other" consciousness. The reference source, in this brand of argument, is usually the community or society. A certain amount of personal freedom must be forfeited for the common good. The component of regulation suggests some curbs on the individual. It is argued that it is in the interest

TABLE SIX

ANTI-ABORTION WITH REGULATION
PATTERN OF ISSUES

Diversity in developmental stages. Fetus is not human neither is it a maternal appendage. Maximization of rights.

Sameness . . . . ▼ . . . . Diversity

Regulations must be flexible enough to consider special circumstances of each case; substantive justice.

Inter-personal : . . ▼ . . . . Impersonal
subjectivity   objectivity

Maximization of rights are strength of pluralistic society; e.g., decriminalization, and insuring safety constitute social improvement.

Improvement . . . . ▼ . . . . Stability

Must consider common good and thus give up some personal rights.

Other- . . . . . . ▼ . . . . Inner-
consciousness   consciousness

The aim to deal with problem in the most efficient and effective manner possible.

Perfectionism . . . . ▼ . . . . Practicality

Final decision is still left to the doctor and the woman.

Sanctioned Duty . . . . ▼ . . . Private Duty

Note: The pattern of issues resembles the Public Interest construct of justice.

138

of society to allow abortion to maximize the expression of rights. It is also in the interest of society to regulate the procedure putting a small restrainer on individual's freedom. Other-consciousness in terms of the common good focuses on the outcome of certain actions. It is in terms of certain social consequences that this position is often justified.

Practicality is also a theme which prevades much of the discussion of the pro-abotion with regulation stance. The recommendations, which are proposed, deal with the problem in the most practical manner possible. Pro-abortion with no restrictions is criticized for being impractical from the standpoint that regulations are necessary to safeguard the best conditions and to discourage unethical abortion mills. Moreover, regulations are intended to prevent the negligent and irresponsible destruction of life. Under the pro-abortion with regulation, there may still be some individuals whose abortion would be deemed illegal. To the degree that some abortions are discouraged, the regulations serve to save some lives that might have been lost had there been no regulations at all. On the other hand, the relative inefficiency of the prohibitive system to placate competing interests, and its overall inability to enforce its standards are among the main criticisms of impracticality which are advance in opposition to the restrictive order.

There is a general concensus among the supporters of the pro-abortion with regulation, that, as the title implies, some sort of regulation is necessary. Nonethless, there is the attitude that in most cases, the final decision must be left to the woman and her physician. Hence, private duty is stressed over sanctioned duty. There is the belief that individual morality will ultimately assure responsible behavior and sensitivity to human needs.

Finally, the goal of the third position on abortion (see Table Seven) seems to be to secure the liberty of each individual to exercise his/her right to the extent that it does not infringe upon the rights of others. The focus of this position is on the individual. Accordingly, we may note that the position approximates the Individual Autonomy construct of justice. The conceptual dimensions which correspond to the Individual Autonomy justice include: sameness; impersonal objectivity; improvement; inner-consciousness; perfectionism; and private duty. It may be remembered that the dimensions of inner-consciousness and perfectionism are unique to this construct.

Similar dimensions may be found in the justification pattern of the pro-abortion without restrictions. For example, the position generally attempts to establish the basic equality of

ANTI-ABORTION WITH NO RESTRICTIONS
PATTERN OF ISSUES

Equal rights of women to control
body - same consideration with
men under the law.

Sameness . . . ● . . . . Diversity

General application - due process under
the Fourtheenth Amendment - upholding
absolute right of women.

Inter-personal . . . . ● . . . . Impersonal
subjectivity   objectivity

Extending equal rights to individuals
constitutes a positive and necessary step
in the progress of civilization.

Improvement . . . . . ● . . . . Stability

Personal well-being and maximization of
personal freedom is goal.

Other- . . . . ● . . . . . Inner-
consciousness   consciousness

Given personal control over life
"century of wanted children" is
possible.

Perfectionism . . . ● . . . . Practicality

Relies on personal accountability.

Sanctioned Duty . . . . ● . . Private Duty

Note: The pattern of issues resembles the Individual
Autonomy construct of justice.

140

women to control their own bodies; thereby indicating the
sameness dimension. And impersonal objectivity may be
inferred from the demand for procedural justice or due process
under the Fourteenth Amendment of the Constitution.

Moreover, it is often argued that the extension of the
individual's right to self-determination is a definite step in the
direction of social justice. The restrictive system is deemed to
be socially repressive. The reformed version is considered to
be an inadequate compromise. The main premise of the pro-
abortion without restrictions position is that individual freedom
constitutes the uncompromised attribute of civilization. Thus,
it is thought to be a step toward the improvement of society.

One of the distinguishing features of this position is that
it is justified in terms of greater individual freedom and extent
of personal rights. The position pays more attention to the
individual motives of the actor rather than to the consequences
of the act. The individual in the sense of an inner
consciousness provides the main reference source of the
pro-abortion with no restrictions stance. Respect for life rises
from the individual's realization of his/her humanity as a
necessary component of self-realization. It is on behalf of the
individual woman rather than on behalf of society or the state
that the arguments are generally structured. The position
suggests that the individual woman comprises the irreducible
and ineffable element in the subject of justice.

Perfectionism, the second unique feature of this position,
is expressed by the idea that given the maximum personal
control over fertility and ultimately one's own life, it is believed
that individuals will duly exercise their freedom, and work
toward a more positive and humane existence. Lader's (1967)
"century of the wanted children" is one example of this
perfectionist's vision. Generally, the position highlights human
virtues rather than exposing the weaknesses.

The obligation to act responsibly, according to the pro-
abortion with no restrictions position, must flow from one's own
moral dictates (private duty). When the abortion decision is
imminent, one is ultimately accountable to oneself.

In summary, then, we may note that there is a certain
degree of overlap among the different positions. They have
two dimensions in common with each of the other positions.
They, also, each exhibit two unique dimensions. Most
importantly, however, there appears to be sufficient evidence in
the literature, that the dilemmas common to the question of
justice, generally, coincide with the dilemmas common to the
specific problem of justice in the abortion controversy (see
Table Eight). The abortion example makes clear that the

141

TABLE EIGHT

Comparison of the Three Alternative positions to the Abortion Dilemma

Conceptual Dimensions of Justice	Fundamental Approaches to the Problem of Abortion		
	Anti-Abortion	Pro-Abortion with regulation	Pro-Abortion with no restrictions
Sameness	■		●
Diversity		▼	
Inter-Personal Subjectivity		▼	
Impersonal Objectivity	■		●
Improvement		▼	●
Stability	■		
Other-Consciousness	■	▼	
Inner-Consciousness			●
Perfectionism			●
Practicality	■	▼	
Sanctioned Duty	■		
Private Duty		▼	●

■ = Normative Conformity;   ▼ = Public Interest;   ● = Individual Autonomy

Note: Each position shares two dimensions with each of the other positions, and has two which are unique to it.

nature of justification reflects the underlying social values and the variable status of conflicts of interest within the society. The analysis of a social issue like abortion reveals how the structure of justice appears in the process of social action.

As a society approaches greater polarity on certain issues, so do the contending claims to justice. The more the conflict is deeply rooted in social values, the more apt the various arguments or counter arguments of the basic positions will appear manifestly improbable or ludicrous to one another. The proponents of the different positions will move away from the substance of logical structure of the various claims to justice. Instead, the confrontation ultimately reaches an emotional impass. The question is how can we go beyond the emotional level and begin to uncover the thought structures involved in social action? Our purpose has been to introduce a line of research related to the sociology of knowledge and social phenomenology, which may be useful for the study of thought structures involving justice in culture.

A particular pattern of conceptual dimensions may be objectively real if it is logically prior to the subjective decision-making process. To answer the question of how the concept of justice affects social decisions or actions, we must consider the following: First, the concept of justice suggests certain sets of social values, which affect the evaluation of actions and future directives. In other words, even though the concept focuses on certain social priorities, it also illuminates certain social problems or shortcomings. This has precise implications for future behavior. Second, it necessitates the comprehension of both the elements which sustain and which subvert the achievement of its expression. In this sense, the thought structures, which may be expressed in the pattern of conceptual dimensions, become functionalized. Their form is dependent on their presumed economic, social and psychological functions or sources. Thus, the analysis of the subjective views which constitute the abortion controversy reveals the structure of justice in social action. Accordingly, the example of the abortion controversy demonstrates that it is a cultural phenomenon which is expressed in society.

Awareness, however, of the entire pattern of conceptual dimensions associated with justice may not always exist in reality. While theoretically, the objective rationality, which is claimed here by the patterns, should approximate or correspond to an individual's or group's position on the issue of abortion, there may be contingent factors which make the identification of a pattern in its entire form difficult to find in any one writer's position. We may recall from the previous chapter that the contingent factors can include any one of the following: (1) The treatment surveys the field and thus provides only

143

sporadic commentary. (2) The treatment only focuses on specialized interest areas (e.g., it brings to bear only medical or only legal considerations, etc.). (3) The treatment attempts to develop a compromise position. (4) The treatment represents only a segregated portion of reality - taken from a specific individual or institutional experience. (5) The treatment does not reach the level of maturity necessary for a full range analysis. Therefore, the works of many individuals espousing similar views are combined to form a general version of the fundamental positions in the abortion controversy.

Representativeness of the authors considered for any one position is assured by an elaborate literature search and cross-reference procedure. By considering general positions rather than the specific views of any one author, a certain degree of objectivity and reliability is maintained. The conceptual dimensions provide the reference points necessary for selecting the information relevant to the issue of justice.

By organizing the various facets of the abortion controversy in terms of the conceptual dimensions of justice, several analytical values may be reaped. In the first place, it is important to note just how limited any one type of argument is. For instance, taking any of the arguments which have been grouped under the sanctioned duty/private duty dilemma, it may be seen that not one is really able to show that abortion laws are justified or not. They, at best, consider the role of morality and law in the decision-making process. Each type of argument advanced usually deals with only one issue or part of the justification of a specific position. For this reason, we should not dismiss or accept a whole position on account of any one argument. It may also mean that there is the possibility of substituting certain features, which are not agreeable, while maintaining some which take personal priority.

Moreover, the presentation seems to demonstrate the necessity of separating out, exactly, what it is that is meant by a certain argument or counter-argument. It is important that we pay attention to the underlying issue, which is addressed, when an argument is advanced. Does the counter-argument appeal to the same basic issue? A great deal of communication may be lost when the opposing viewpoints are posited on different levels.

It is also imperative that the precise nature of the disagreement is noted. For example, do the positions on a particular issue differ dramatically; that is, appearing on opposite ends of the continuum. Or do they merely represent the question of interpretation?

Finally, the patterns or objective reference points of the various justifications of abortion may be instrumental in some conflict resolution. By visually representing different attitudinal systems, we may quickly uncover the points of departure, as well as the common ground. Once the common ground can be established it may be easier to approach the areas of conflict.

The abortion controversy provides, we think, an interesting example of conflict-resolution. While this has not been the purpose of our conceptual scheme, this application is interesting.

At the time when the American Courts were considering recommendations of the American Law Institute to legally extend the criteria for abortion, Congressman Rev. Robert Drinan, who, up to this point, strongly supported the basic anti-abortion position, retorted with a paper entitled "The Right of the Fetus to be Born" (1967-68). What is especially interesting in this work is that it suggests a very important shift in emphasis; and subsequently a division in the anti-abortion position.

Drinan argues that it would be preferable to have no laws governing abortion, if the only alternative is moderate laws. He develops the argument in the following manner. First, he holds that abortion is immoral, since it disregards "the right of the fetus to be born." Second, there are two alternatives under the deliberation of the Courts: (1) no laws; and (2) moderate laws. Third, moderate laws are tantamount to a State's indulgence of the killing of human beings for reasons of inconvenience. Therefore, he concludes that the alternative of no law is better. It is better to leave the State neutral than committed to a justification of killing (1967-68).

Drinan's conclusion essentially represents a shift from sanctioned duty to private duty, which signifies a move in the direction of conflict resolution. Abandoning the demand for the legal prohibition of abortion constitutes a major concession. This, of course, is not to say that Drinan did not run up against a great deal of opposition. Some anti-abortionists would not accept such a compromise. There are, however, those who agree. Margaret Mead (1982) suggested that "both partners can in good conscience vote for the repeal of laws governing abortion and place abortion under the medical profession, and under the Churches who may educate their own members and work to convert non-members to their point of view" (1). Support even came from the officials of the Roman Catholic Church, who with Drinan, reassessed their positions and concluded that laws are not absolutely crucial to the preservation of the principles of the church. Cardinal Cushing of Boston confirms that Catholic moral principles do not need the support of law (GAP, 1970: 25). By going over to the side of private duty, Drinan suggests a way to alleviate some of the pressure of the conflict.

Perhaps, by presenting the various conflict positions in terms of the conceptual dimensions of justice, we may begin to unearth ways in which the contrasts may be diminished, without actually relinquishing one's fundamental ideals. Perhaps, with a concrete representation of the logical course of certain basic positions, we may predict certain arguments. This approaches the problem of attitude change more rationally. It avoids motivating change on the basis of attacking a few random arguments.

While each position has certain weak as well as strong points, each offers a coherent and legitimate claim to justice. Callahan (1970) aptly states:

> To see one side or the other as representing pure progress or pure decline misses the point. The positions of all sides represent progress, though progress in different directions. To say this is not necessarily to point the way to a resolution of conflict, but it is at least to cut the ground from under those who would represent their opponents as moral barbarians (8).

Chapter Six

THE VALUE OF THE CONCEPTUAL
SCHEME OF JUSTICE
FOR
SOCIOLOGICAL UNDERSTANDING

A.   Other Applications of the Conceptual Model.

In the previous chapter, the problem of justice in the abortion decision is used to illustrate the application of the conceptual scheme.   We outline the basic positions constituting the abortion controversy and relate them to each of the pairs of conceptual dimensions of justice.   Our conclusions suggest that the three basic positions of the abortion dilemma (i.e., anti-abortion, pro-abortion with regulation, and pro-abortion with no restrictions) correspond to the patterns of the three constructs of justice (i.e., Normative Conformity, Public Interest, and Individual Autonomy), respectively.   The treatment exposes the underlying value systems which influence the decision of justice when the abortion question is raised.

There is always the possibility that the one example picked for the illustration of the conceptual scheme is somehow unique in its expression of the justice themes.   In order to demonstrate the existence of the themes in other contexts, it may be important to briefly examine a few other examples.   We show only in a cursory way the appearance of the themes of justice in such problems as punishment and censorship.   Some application to international justice is also noted.

The Justification of Punishment

Every known society demonstrates some sort of system of punishment.   This system enforces the established social organization and reinforces its specific values.   In contemporary societies punishment is part of a formal legal system.   It is usually considered only when there is a distinct infraction of the legal codes - the implication being that the deviation is willful and intended by the actor.

The philosophy of punishment includes various interpretations (or ideologies).   Holding true to a sociology of knowledge interpretation, these ideologies periodically shift from time to time (historically and contemporarily) depending on numerous factors (e.g., the strength of a scientific community, the current "crime rate", etc.. See Kuhn, 1970). For purposes of analysis we may distinguish three distinct types of punishment ideologies: (1) theories which are concerned with the notion of deterrence; (2) theories which focus on the idea of reformation; and (3) theories which depend on the basic concepts of retribution. By superimposing the question of justice on the basic conceptions of punishment, we may begin to uncover the essential value systems and areas of discord which are inherent in their justifications.

In the first sense, punishment is justified on the grounds that it serves the purpose of protecting society. It assures respect for the legal order. The function of punishment from this point of view is simply deterrence. Kelson (1957), for example, suggests that "the law of the state, like the law of nature" must be "freed from the myth of retribution." Punishment, according to Kelsen, must not be justified in terms of some abstract purpose, but on the basis of a concrete and clear reason (312).

Clear articulation of the consequences of legal deviation and the degree of certainty with which the law is enforced, go hand in hand with the ultimate power of deterrence punishment. Beginning with the Age of Reason in the 18th Century, the aim of criminal law has gradually shifted from punishment for its own sake to punishment as a means of improving social behavior (Newman, 1978). Punishment is designed to deter future crime by drawing attention to or making an example of the deviant. While specific deterrence may take place, i.e., the deviant learns from his or her mistakes and may not deviate in the future, general deterrence is not concerned with the convict but with the public at large (Van den Haag, 1975). The punishment of the offender serves, theoretically, as an example for the rest of us. Thus, "deterrence protects the social order by restraining not the actual offender, who - eo ipso, has not been deterred but other members of society, potential offenders, who still can be deterred" (61).

As Sutherland and Cressey (1978) note, there seems to be no question that if punitive terror is great enough, most people will fear the punishers and will conform (336). However, the hundreds of studies devoted to the general deterrence notion have usually addressed a more narrow question, viz., whether existing punishment systems significantly affect existing crime rates (Sutherland and Cressey, 1978, 22). The challenge then becomes one of whether officials can control criminality by creating the "degree of terror" needed to control it and no more. Through criminal (and civil) law and its sanctions, law makers seek to calculate the appropriate amounts of pain to inflict on law transgressors, thus convincing bystanders that the costs of committing a crime outweigh the benefits.

The general deterrence principle is often stated in economic or practical terms (e.g., debt to society) such that it is assumed that people, criminals and non-criminals, make rational choices about those activities which maximize gains and minimize losses (Palmer, 1977).

Although deterrence theory has been cast in economic, as well as political and sociological terms, the processes involved in general deterrence appear to be psychological in nature (Geerken and Gove, 1975). Concepts such as the celerity, certainty and severity of punishment are factors that potential law violators must take into consideration. More importantly, while specific punishments may have little influence on deterring specific individuals from committing specific crimes, the existence of a criminal code with penal sanctions more than likely has a negative effect on the development of criminal ideologies. E. A. Ross succinctly states this point:

> Not the crimes punished, but the crimes prevented should measure the worth of the law....If out of a score of law-abiding persons, only one obeys the law from the fear of its penalties, it does not follow that the penal system occupies a correspondingly insignificant place among the supports of social order. For the rules of the social game are respected by the many good men chiefly because they are forced upon the few bad. If the one rascal among twenty men might aggress at will, the higher forms of control would break down, the fair play instinct would cease to bind, and, between bad example and the impulse of retaliation, man after man would be detached from the honest majority. Thus, the deadly contagion of lawlessness would spread with increasing rapidity till the social order lay in ruins. The law, therefore, however minor its part of given moment in the actual coercion of citizens, is still the cornerstone of the edifice of order (1916: 25).

Before a reformation (or medical model) philosophy of punishment became popular and general deterrence was regarded as the principal purpose of punishment, criminal penalities and their execution were made as public and brutal as possible (e.g., public hangings). The purpose of such affairs was to expose the public to the most visible forms of power of the state (See Foucault, 1979). Even today, when a community experiences (or perceives) an increase in criminality, they react by demanding that more swift and severe sanctions be applied.

149

Perhaps the most extreme "test" of the general deterrence ideology is the debate over capital punishment. Based on several differing methodologies regarding the value of the death penalty as a deterrent, the evidence to date shows a relatively unimportant relationship between the murder rate and the death penalty (See Dike, 1982 for the most current studies). Such evidence, however, fails to dampen the public's interest periodically in the use of capital punishment as a crime deterrent.

The greater the ability of the individual to clearly comprehend and predict detection, conviction and the nature of sentencing, the more likely the process will have deterrent power and assure conformity to the legal dictates. The emphasis on clearly defined objective criteria (i.e., laws) and the concern over the preservation of society, sanctioned obligation, economic or practical considerations, etc., remind one of the Normative Conformity construct of justice.

The second basic conception of punishment focuses on a reformation process which attempts to maximize individual's alternatives of behavior within the structure of law. Ultimately, the individual is left with the choice to obey or not to obey. The ability of different individuals to make the proper choices and the range of legitimate choices permitted by the social structure compose the main questions of this perspective. If the range of legitimate alternatives are insufficient or unaccessible by some individuals, in the sense of the maximization of individual freedom to choose, reform of either the individual or the social structure is imminent. From this perspective the system of punishment can only be justified to the extent that it influences the social readaptation of the deviant.

The reformation or rehabilitation ideology, often referred to as the "treatment model" has paralleled the rise of modern social science (e.g., psychology) (Thornton, James, Doerner, 1982). While at one point in time reform involved literally "beating the devil" out of law violators, we now see criminal behavior as just another manifestation of pathology that can assumedly be controlled by some form of therapeutic activity. Therapy may include efforts to change the "offender's intent, motivation or even character toward law abiding conduct" (Van den Haag, 1975: 58). The criminal, via the medical model, may be reclassified as a "sick" individual who, once treated, can return to a functional role in society. Treatment procedures are as varied as the imagination of the social scientists who conceives them. Various therapies may approximate punishment in their design and application but the final outcome (assumedly a "reformed" individual) is different. Thus, for instance, hard manual labor instills a "work ethic" in the individual or behavioral therapy using negative reinforcement schedules, alters inappropriate behavioral responses.

The rise of correctional institutions in Western society generally parallels our notions about treatment (Allen & Simonsen, 1981). Rather than prisons simply being holding houses for the punishment of law violators, per se, they became conceived of as places of confinement to identify and treat the transgressors' problems (See Mitford, 1973). The needs of the institution often take precedence over the needs of the individual, and treatment programs fail to function adequately. There are many who question whether any treatment can take place within an institutional setting. They use high recidivist rates as support for their arguments. As a result, the community corrections movement has gained support in recent years.

Reformation is ultimately justified by its actual effect on society. Hobhouse (1949) notes that the concept of punishment "is a mechanical and dangerous means of protection which requires the greatest wisdom and humanity to convert into an agency of reform" (128). Punishment functions to adjust the individual behavior or social conditions in order to assure the future selection of appropriate behavior. The reformist position attempts to maximize all the rights of all the parties concerned: Society's right as well as the prisoner's rights are considered. The position centers around the notion of social well-being. Reform constitutes improvement in society and more humane treatment of society's transgressors. The position seems to closely resemble the Public Interest construct of justice.

The third fundamental type of theory of punishment centers on the belief that punishment must not be imposed for any instrumental reasons, as assuring certain social consequences. Rather, it is justified on the grounds that individuals must be held responsible for their actions and accept their just deserts. Kant articulates this basic orientation when he writes the following:

> Juridical punishment can never be administered merely as a means for promoting another good, either with regard to the criminal himself or to civil society, but must in all cases be imposed because the individual may meet with the fate which his deeds deserve and the guilt of blood may not rest upon the people (Ginsberg, 1965: 174).

Punishment is not designed to protect society from aberrations. It does not focus on reform or the social effects of punishment. This perspective underscores the psychological necessity of holding individuals responsible for their transgressions or misdeeds. Dostoevsky's novel, <u>Crime and Punishment</u> (1951), perhaps, represents one of the most vivid statements of this basic perspective. Roskolkov, Dostoevsky's main character, yearns to be punished for his crime. He considers it his right. While this fundamental view is attached to the idea of atonement or the idea of cleansing the soul, it does <u>not</u> include the notion of revenge.

The most important feature of this interpretation is that the crime must be rendered <u>void</u>, not so much on the grounds that it produces undesirable social consequences, but because it constitutes an invasion of the rights of other individuals. In this sense, punishment is not held as a means to a certain end. Punishment in the retributive sense, then, is not intended as an intimidation, but as an act of the cancellation of inner guilt and the misdeed itself.

This philosophy has its roots in many different historical periods throughout the world. Punishment, once a form of immediate and personal retribution, administered by the victim or his kin, has evolved to a matter handled by the State, whereby the component of revenge became nullified for the good of the whole. To fully understand punishment, however, we have to follow the evolution of the concept from its primitive origins and also follow it from the evolution of religion, because various forms of religion have been champions of punishment throughout the ages (Newman, 1978). Early forms of punishment, for example, were expressly designed to rid the community of some form of pollution manifested by the offender. Under early Mosaic law, certain crimes which aroused the anger of God, such as blasphemy and idolatry, were punished by stoning the offender to death. Stones, were so to speak, missiles of individual sins transferred to the criminal. By stoning the individual, Hebrew society cleansed itself of the polluting criminal but also cleansed itself of its own sins.

From another view, punishment can also be seen as a right, like any other. Morality ultimately derives from the individual consciousness of the right thing to do. Wrongdoers can only be set on the right course through their own acceptance of the misdeed and their willingness to assume full responsibility for their actions. Moral behavior in the future cannot be assured by frightening the individual, but rather through the process of personal contrition and reacceptance of the legal code formerly disregarded. The implication is that punishment as a social reaction can only be successful if the individual submits voluntarily to it. Following it, the belief is that the individual is totally absolved of the misdeed. In many respects, retributive punishment, even in its harshest forms, treats offenders as individuals or at least as potential moral beings, thus having some possible advantage over rehabilitative punishment. The distinct focus on the individual right and individual responsibility, humanism and autonomy, which is evident in this basic orientation, encompasses the Individual Autonomy construct of justice.

It appears then, that looking at the values associated with the concept of punishment, different constructs of justice may be relevant. The conceptual scheme may be employed to enhance the understanding of the dynamics of the different theories of punishment. Of course, our effort to connect the constructs of justice with the basic concepts of punishment is very general and highly tentative. The problem is complex and deserves a great deal more depth. The next step is to test the "goodness of fit" of the various theories of punishment to our conceptual dimensions of justice.

The Justification of Censorship

We suggest that other areas can also be studied from our justice dimensions. The question of the relationship of justice to censorship, we think, is a pertinent topic.

Since the beginning of civilization, censorship has served as a prudential conservative method of preventing moral or political confusion and the ultimate destruction of the organization of society. Whether in theory or in practice, all known societies have exercised some degree of control over the social behavior or attitudes of its members. Traditionally, socieites have held individuals subversive if they undermined the predominate value systems (i.e., the expression of the prevailing ethics, religion, or the general beliefs concerning the nature of the human personality, basic human rights, and the established social order). The responsibility of censorship has, historically, been assumed by religious leaders, by the State, and frequently by unofficial members of society.

While the concept of censorship appears to be operative in some sense, in every society, it is usually the subject of conflict and debate. The issue of justice in censorship broadly concerns, on the one hand, the legitimacy of authority to demand conformity. On the other hand, it raises the issues of the right to defiance and individual judgment. The extent of technological development and the level of civilization have presented the twentieth century with a particular dilemma concerning the justification of a position on censorship. Given the incredible power of communication to motivate change or influence great masses of people, and the general effects of modernization on social existence, never before in the history of the world have so many individuals been so vulnerable to immediate and arbitrary manipulation or subjugation. People living within relatively isolated social units (e.g., nuclear families), existing under the comparatively artificial conditions of urban environments, and having few roots in the past may be particularly open to the domination of the contagion of external opinion. The works of David Riesman (1953), The Lonely Crowd, and Richard Weaver (1953), The Ethics of Rhetoric, are especially relevant in this context. Riesman's "other-directed persons" refer to individuals who rely on the approval of other people for support of their own values and of themselves. There is implied in an "other-directedness" a tyranny over the independence of individual judgment. The "other", then, may provide a vehicle for censorship sometimes subtle and sometimes obvious over nearly every aspect of human interaction.

Similarly, Weaver indicates a tyranny of words by bringing attention to "god terms" and "charismatic terms" which are words assuming special meaning and motive power. These words call for immediate approval or disapproval irrespective of the context in which they are found (e.g., tradition, communism, totalitarianism, pragmatism, atheism, value judgment, and scientific). There is a general fear in the United States and in the world that individuals who rest on the notion that nothing should be censored may fall prey to a type of censorship more inflexible than can be imagined.

For example, the Soviet Union at its inception was boastful over its abolition of control over private affairs. Yet in the wake of this emancipation, it reverted to a censorship which is enforced by an elaborate system of law and state propaganda so pervasive that it attempts to ideologically direct many interpersonal relationships including parent/child and husband/wife relationships. It even tries to restrict personal spiritual experience by curtailing certain religious expression.

The present potential magnitude of force and efficiency of censorship is unmatched by any historical epic. This age is also unique in demonstrating with some success that a society does not necessarily have to have any formal mode of censorship (e.g., Sweden). Justice is complicated by the fact that while sometimes the role of censorship as a cohesive and protective element in the social order is necessary, it may result in repression.

The issue of justice in the problem of censorship focuses on two basic questions: First, can the moral and political fabric of society sustain the lack of any censorship over time? And, second, are there any proper limits or methods of censorship which will protect individuals from the extreme degree of repression that is presently possible to attain?

Without attempting the depth of analysis necessary to understand this very complicated problem, there appear to be generally three ways of dealing with this problem. First, there is the position which suggests that once voluntary censorship is condemned, the way is open to repressive consequences. The underlying assumption is that morality and social cohesiveness cannot be accomplished externally. This can only result from internal self-determination and the individual consciousness of the essential interdependence among humans in society. Even in its brief form, this position approaches the Individual Autonomy construct of justice.

The second position advocates relatively mild regulation as the stipulation of certain guidelines: age restrictions, system of codes for ready assessment, and the establishment of informal censorship boards, etc. Regulations are usually designed to serve the social good. Their essential purpose is to maximize the rights of both the society to express its interests, and at the same time the rights of individuals to ultimately make self-judgments. Accordingly, this general orientation corresponds closely to the Public Interest construct of justice.

Finally, there are those who insist that only through strict control and a formal system of prohibitions can individuals be protected from any creeping onslaught of repressive subjugation by undesirable or foreign bodies. Only via strict control can the social order be secured and the expression of certain individual rights be protected from invasion or abuse. Following, this position approximates the Normative Conformity construct of justice.

Of course, the present association of the positions in the censorship controversy and the constructs of justice are highly speculative. Intuitively, there do appear to be comparable themes. However, as with punishment, we need to compare the different facts of the controversy with the conceptual dimensions of justice to see if there is enough similarity in patterns to warrant such a connection.

International Justice

The entanglement of justice issues with the problems of society are manifested not only in various alignments on domestic questions, but even more momentously on the vaster stage of international relations. Perhaps, the outstanding need of present civilization is the attainment of an international justice. At the current time, for example, the mode of justice, which appears to characterize the international level is the Individual Autonomy construct ("individual" refers to individual nations of the world). Generally, justice in the international domain seems particularly intent upon articulating a primary concern with interference or domination by other nations. It is a recent innovation that the task of determining "equitable distribution of conditions of well-being for all", or in other words, a Public Interest version of justice, has been considered in international justice ("public" refers to world society). There is also a movement toward establishing an international justice through the organization of a central body of control (world government) and a system of enforcement of strict prohibitions, in order to secure world order and peace i.e., Normative Conformity).

Future Implications of the Conceptual Model

Considering that there are different conceptions of justice, we may posit a comparative study of different institutions or even cultures, as well as the analysis of different motivating systems inherent in controversial issues or social problems involving justice. We may begin by addressing the following questions: On what level and with what different social, historical and psychological conditions does one find different definitions of justice? What variations may be found among the value systems or goals associated with different modes of justice? What social indicators are associated with such differences? When does one find nothing to which justice usefully applies?

It is proposed that from a sociological perspective, we need not seek to establish amid the great plurality of opinions, visions, and debate any definite constraints or universals to constitute all decisions or actions involving the questions of justice. Sociologically, the real significance of the clarification of such a concept of justice lies in its potential to add to the comprehensibility and lucidity of the social issues and the motivations which underlie certain types of interaction and decisions.

Justice is an important sociological concept because it is not merely restricted to limited contexts. The concept of justice transcends specific contexts, since it implies qualities which are not context bound. Accordingly, the idea of justice may underlie the existence of social institutions themselves (i.e., the justification (criteria) behind the purpose of establishing particular institutions, or the justification for imposing and maintaining certain social values).

To this end, the concept of justice assumes an instrumentalistic character. If justice, in the sense of social purpose, is considered instrumental in uncovering the motive behind human association and social institutionalization, the way is open to employing the method for reevaluation and reform in existing social structures. For example, with all the pressing problems of society, it is very important to consider how various expressions of justice may affect the future.

We cannot merely ask what is needed by individuals in a particular society or community. We must, in addition, ask what is going to happen to the society or community once certain changes are implemented. How will the changes affect all the interested parties or modes of interaction? How will conflict be resolved? The constructs of justice may be generally understood in terms of a decision-making process in goal attainment. Justice becomes an issue everytime a new innovation or type of community is integrated into a particular social structure. How are the constructs of justice institutionally expressed within society? Can the models be used for intervention to influence attitudes or actions? For instance, what will happen when a particular model of justice is introduced into the curriculum of a law school or a graduate school of sociology?

The extent of utility of the conceptual scheme of justice for sociological investigation can be far reaching. The conceptual scheme developed here provides a way of looking at social institutions and social problems in general. Depending on the particular frame of reference, whether it be Normative Conformity, Public Interest or Individual Autonomy, a myriad of special questions and values as well as problems are indicated. Each mode of justice, with its accompanying pattern of dimensions, evokes a special insight into the values involved in the adjustment of social relations and at the same time it suggests the possible area of breakdown in social relations. Each implies the awareness of the necessity of choice between incompatible values.

Finally, the conceptual scheme of justice deals with various problems which may, perhaps, be extended or developed into a field of knowledge. The following areas have been considered in greater or lesser degree in this book:

(1) Knowledge of reasons or conditions why the study of justice has become urgent.

(2) Knowledge of the key social, economic, and technological trends likely to significantly influence or be influenced by certain resolutions of justice.

(3) Knowledge of beginning level of structural elements and components of the concept of justice.

(4) Knowledge of the variety of justice resolutions and the experiences associated in several of the more popular outcomes.

(5) Knowledge of the sources of information or the tradition connected with various resolutions of justice.

(6) Knowledge and working use of vocabulary and values connected with certain notions of justice.

(7) Knowledge of assumptions held about particular definitions of justice; implications of holding these assumptions (especially the implications on structure and human beings).

(8) Knowledge of application and limitations of certain concepts of justice.

(9) Knowledge of other ideas connected with the concept of justice and the variety of ways they may be expressed in different definitions.

(10) Knowledge of social indicators which may be associated with a commitment to certain justice resolutions.

The relationship between justice and economic activity, political activity, ethical or prudential values are obviously not simple ones. Indeed, sometimes the very achievement of certain justice goals raises new possibilities of injustice. Justice cannot be understood merely in the light of some temporary placation of conflicting value systems or standards. And to imply that justice essentially reduces to a reflection of the political or economic power structures is to focus on only a small portion of the denotative meaning of justice.

Theoretical constructs of justice may facilitate an understanding of some of the most critical and inflamed issues in modern history. The extent to which these debated issues are limited to heated emotional controversy, understanding or resolution can hardly be approached in sociological terms.

B. Epilogue: Justice and Progress

Justice shows its intimate and most far-reaching relevance to the principles and problems of human living. Justice involves <u>choice</u> and the organization of the values in human conduct. The problematic of justice reflects the question: Is humankind really capable of genuine rational choice? As the problem of choice in justice probes the moral resources of the individual, so the ultimate problem of the progress toward justice demonstrates the moral capacity of human civilization in its historical development.

Perhaps, progress in civilization may be understood in terms of the expanding range of values which are available for the realization of justice. But civilization may demonstrate both the heights humankind can attain, and the depth it can sink. Ironically, the prospects of a higher and vaster achievement presents one with the risk of a more stupendous failure. The present age manifests this aspect of civilization in world wide terms.

The traditional failure of the realization of justice or the history of injustice, however, must <u>not</u> be used as an indictment of the concept of justice. Rather, the injustices must be taken as warnings aginst the casual abandonment or the cynical distortion of an intrinsic quality of civilization.

We must not confuse vehicles for potential social knowledge of justice with justice itself. We must not confuse the range of choices for potential decisions with the decision itself. It seems that the age long quest for a standard of "better justice" ultimately suggests that individuals have a mistrust of their own judgment. An over-reliance on a standard of "better decision-making" may actually impede people's confidence in this own ability to decide or choose for themselves. It may even enfeeble their belief that they can decide. Perhaps, it is when individuals un-learn how to make decisions concerning justice on their own evidence, that the society becomes a victim of injustice.

The long general abandonment in society for value judgments has been supported by social institutions. For example, our educational system in the United States generally exhibits little concern in the curriculum for value decisions. The supposed focus on the standard of the objective or the scientific value-free orientation is often misconstrued to preclude the treatment or expression of values. Knowledge or science is frequently defined to mean an institutional enterprise of experts, rather than the rational decision-making or creativity of human beings. Little wonder, then, that there appears to be a general loss of confidence in humankind's ability to attain the levels of achievement in civilization necessary to accomodate such a concept as justice.

Contemporary Western culture represents a strange enigma. In the presence of the marvelous achievements of science and technology and art, which humankind has put forth to subdue the limitless forces of nature, it appears that only a relatively moderate amount of effort ought to supply inexhaustable abundance and benefit for the population of the world. Yet these splendid feats of achievement have not - as John Stuart Mill so cogently expressed - been able to mitigate one human woe. Instead, now for the first time in human history, nature stands helpless before humankind. That the idea of progress stands perplexed and confused before this enigma can only indicate that the notion of progress in civilization has been misconceived. Rather than focusing on technology and science to provide a standard for the "better life", it is time to be concerned with how we can "progress" to a more humane or desirable human being. We may wonder whether there would have been any substantive difference in the development of Western civilization, had the ancients who posed the question of ultimate good provided the model for intellectual pursuit, instead of those ancients who sought to find the answer to ultimate truth?

The idea that progress without a concern for the value of justice can be "engineered" is part of a misconception. The ability of present institutions to arbitrarily define such values as education, welfare, success, quality of leadership, or justice are also part of the misconception.

The recent surge of interest in the concept of justice may indicate that people are leary of organization without justice or accountability and the rational decision-making process this entails. Only when we can understand the concept of justice not as the central mythical ideology of industrial societies, but as the motivating force in civilization, can we explain our deep concern. Only then can we understand the complex web of values surrounding it, and its connection with the self-image of the contemporary individual and the society.

We believe that the present effort can stimulate an interest in a sociological examination of how values function in society. The conflicts among values in society mirror the difficulties involved in conceptualizing justice and in socially administering it. As society approaches greater polarity on certain issues, so do the contending claims of justice.

NOTES

1. Piaget expressed this same idea when he discussed how children learn about justice in his The Moral Judgement of the Child (1982).

2. The terms "ideation", "evaluation", "prescription" are not Plato's. They are used by the present investigators with the intent to summarize the substance of what Plato suggested in his Republic.

3. Plato's Republic seems to be an attempt by Plato to develop a whole metaphysics in order to deal with this problem of the acquisition of social knowledge.

4. See Allport, Vernon, and Lindsey (1960); Brandt (1971); Kluckhone and Strodtbeck (1971); Parsons (1964) and Pepper (1958).

5. Although the persistence of some values and ideas throughout history may support arguments for a universal hierarchy of values or ideas which is distinct from social reality (e.g., Green, 1901) there is no attempt made here to support such a position.

6. Hammurabi's Code. Yale University References Manuscripts, n.d.

7. Aristotle labelled these concepts "themis" and "dike" respectively. For further discussion see Del Vecchio (1956).

8. This all human criterion in Marxist ethics is also developed in Howard Selsam's Socialism and Ethics. New York: International Publishers, 1943.

9. See Aristotle's definition of spontaneity and the connection to justice in Nicomeachean Ethics 1168 (28) and 1169 (18).

10. For an example of this, see R. Pound's Social Control Through Law, Archon Books, 1968, p. 16.

11. John Robinson, J. Rusk and K. Head. Measures of Political Attitudes. Ann Arbor: MI. Institute for Social Research, Survey Research Center, 1969.

    The scale reviewed in the section on Democratic principles provide intriguing

161

evidence of the non-ideological nature of American attitudes toward democratic principles and the specific instances of their application. Americans, especially the less affluent, have been found to be intolerant of specific groups (such as deviants and non-conformists) and in specific situations. At the same time almost all Americans have professed belief in the general principles of democracy and tolerance.

12. The Court's inadequacy in fully explaining the right to privacy concept and its full implications rests on a long line of cases which have likewise been very general in their interpretation. Several pre-Roe lower court decisions struck down abortion statutes for imparing the right to privacy escaped legal analysis. In most of these cases, proponents of abortion argued mechanically "that abortion involves both family and sex, and that Griswold v Connecticut (381 U.S. 479 (1965) and Eisenstadt v Baird (405 U.S. 438 (1972) place a zone of privacy around such matters" (Schneider and Vinovskis, 1980: 165-166). One of the first cases to declare an abortion statute unconstitutional, People v Belous (71 Cal. 2d 954, 458 P. 2d 194, 80 Ca. Rptr. 354 (1969), cert. denied, 397 U.S. 915 (1970) follows the lower court's reasoning.

The fundamental right of the woman to choose whether to bear children follows from the Supreme Court's and this court's repeated acknowledgement of a "right to privacy" or "liberty" in matters related to marriage, family and sex... that such a right is not enumerated in either the United States or California consitutions is no impediment to the existence of the right (71 Cal. 2d at 963, 458 P. 2d at 199-200, 80 Cal. Rptr. at 359-360).

BIBLIOGRAPHY

A.C.L.U. cited in The Right to Abortion by The Group for the Advancement of Psychiatry (G.A.P.). New York: Charles Scribners Sons, 1970, p. 27.

Abbott, Everett. Justice and The Modern Law. Boston: Houghton Mifflin, 1913.

Acton, H. B. "Distributive Justice, the Invisible Hand and The Cunning Reason," Political Studies, 20: 421-31, December, 1972.

Albee, L. A. A History of English Utilitarianism. London: Swan Sonnenschein, 1902.

Allen, H. E. and C. E. Simonsen. Corrections in America. New York: Macmillan, 1981.

Allport, G; Vernon, P; Lindsey, G. A Study of Values. (3rd ed) Boston: Houghton Mifflin, 1960.

Almond, Gabriel and Bingham Powell. Comparative Politics-Developmental Approach. Boston: Little Brown, 1966.

American Friends Service Committee. Who Shall Live? Man's Control Over Birth and Death. New York: Hill and Wang, 1970.

American Journal of Obstetrics and Gynecology, "A Statement on Abortion by One Hundred Professors of Obstetrics," American Journal of Obstetrics and Gynecology, 112: 992-998, 1, April, 1972.

American Law Institute. Model Penal Code. Philadelphia: American Law Institute, July 30, 1962.

American Medical Association, "Special Issue: Medicolegal Aspects of Abortion," The Citation, 24: 65-80, 15, December 1971.

Andenaes, Johannes. Punishment and Deterrence. Ann Arbor: University of Michigan Press, 1974.

Angell, Robert. Free Society and the Moral Crisis. Lansing: University of Michigan, 1958.

Aquinas, Thomas. Summa Theologiae. Ottawa: Institute of Medieval Studies of Ottawa, 1941-1945.

Aristotle cited in "Egalitarianism and the Ideal of Equality," by Hugo Adam Bedan in Equality by Pennock and J. Chapan (eds) New York: Atherton Press, 1967, p. 18.

Aristotle cited in Ginsberg's On Justice in Society. Ithaca, New York: Cornell University Press, 1965, p. 7.

Aristotle. The Nicamachean Ethics. Trans. by F. H. Peters. London: Kegan, Paul, French Toubner and Co., 1891.

Aristotle. The Politics of Aristotle. Oxford, 1887-1902. (W. L. Newman, editor, 4 volumes; translated by E. Barker, 1946).

Arrow, K., "Some Ordinalistic-Utilitarian Notes on Rawl's Theory of Justice", J. Philos., 70: 245-63, May 10, 1973.

Arrow, Kenneth. Social Choice and Individual Values. New York: Wiley, 1951.

Ash, William. Marxism and Moral Concepts. New York: Monthly Review Press, 1964.

Austin, J. The Province of Jurisprudence Determined. H. I. A. Hart, (ed) London: Weidenfeld and Nicolson, 1954.

Baldwin, R. W. Social Justice. Oxford: Pergamon Press, 1966.

Bardis, P. D., "Abortion and Public Opinion: A Research Note," Journal of Marriage and The Family, 34: 111, February 1972.

Barry, Brain. The Liberal Theory of Justice. Oxford: Clarendon Press, 1973.

Barth, K. "The Protection of Life" In E. Batchelor. Abortion: The Moral Issues. New York: Pilgrim Press, 1982.

Beck, M. D., "Abortion: The Mental Health Consequences of Unwantedness," Seminars in Psychiatry, 2: 263-274, August 1970.

Beck, M. D. "The Destiny of the Unwanted Child: The Issue of Compulsory Pregnancy," Abortion and The Unwanted Child. California Committee on Therapeutic Abortion. Carl Reiterman (ed)., New York: Springer, 1971.

Bedau, Hugo. "Justice and Classical Utilitarianism", in Friedrich & Chapman Justice Nomos VI, 1963.

Bedau, Hugo. "Egalitarianism and the Ideal of Equality," in Pennock and Chapman, Equality, 1967.

Bentham, J. An Introduction to the Principles of Morals and Legislation. L. J. Lafleur, (ed) New York: Hafner, 1961.

Berger, Peter and Thomas Luckman. The Social Construction of Reality: A Treatise in the Sociology of Knowledge. Garden City, N. J.: Doubleday, 1966.

Berlin, Sir Isaiah, "Rationality of Value Judgments" in Friedrich (ed) Ration Decision.

Berman, H. Justice in Russia. Cambridge: Harvard University Press, 1950.

Bernard, Jessie. Women and The Public Interest. New York: Atherton, 1971.

Bershady, Harold. Ideology and Social Knowledge. Boston: Porter Sargent Publishers, 1973.

Birnbaum, Norman, "The Sociological Analysis of Ideologies (1940-1960): A Trend Report and Bibliography," Current Sociology, IX, 2, 1960.

Blake, J., "Abortion and Public Opinion: The 1960-1970 Decade," Science 17: 540-549, February 12, 1971.

Blau, Peter. Approaches to the Study of Social Structures. New York: Free Press, 1975.

Bogdan, Robert and Steven Taylor. Introduction to Qualitative Research Methods: A Phenomenological Approach to the Social Sciences. New York: Wiley, 1975.

Bosserman, Philip. Dialectical Sociology. New York: MacMillan and Co., 1964.

Bradley, F. H. Ethical Studies. London: 1876

Bradley, F. H. See Jeremiah Newman. Conscience Versus

165

Law. Chicago: Franciscan Herald Press, 1971.

Brandt, R. Value and Obligation: Systematic Readings in Ethics. New York: Harcout, 1971.

Brecht, Arnold. "Relative and Absolute Justice" in M. D. Forkosch (ed) The Political Philosophy of Arnold Becht, 1954.

Brentano, Franz. The Foundation and Construction of Ethics. Trans. by E. H. Schneewind. London: Routledge and Kegan Paul, 1973.

Brentano, Franz. The Origin of the Knowledge of Right and Wrong. Trans. by C. Hague. London: A Constable, 1902.

Broad, C. D. Five Types of Ethical Theory. London: Routledge and Kegan Paul, 1962.

Brody, Baruch. Abortion and the Sanctity of Human Life: A Philosophical View. Cambridge, Mass.: M.I.T. Press, 1975.

Bosserman, Phillip. Dialectical Sociology: An Analysis of the Sociology of George Gurvitch. Boston: Porter Sargent Publishers, 1968.

Brunner, E. Justice and the Social Order. Trans. by Mary Hottinger, New York: Harper and Brothers, 1945.

Brunton, J. A., "Egoism and Morality," Philosophical Quarterly, 6: 289-303, 1956.

Bruyn, Severyn., "Notes on Justice: A Category of Social Research and Theory", unpublished paper. Boston College, n. d.

Buchanan, J. M., "Hobbesian Interpretation of the Raulsian Difference Principle," Kyklos, 29, No. 1: 5-25, 1976.

Cahn, E. The Sense of Injustice: An Anthropocentric View of Law. New York: University Press, 1949, 151.

Caldera, R., "Universal Common Good and International Social Justice," trans. by J. Tello, R. Pol. 38: 27-39, January, 1976.

Callahan, Daniel. Abortion: Law, Choice and Morality. New York: MacMillan, 1970.

166

Campbell, T. D., "Humanity Before Justice," British Journal Political Science, 4: 1-16, January, 1974.

Cardozo, B. N. Growth of the Law, 1924.

Carr, E. H. Karl Marx: A Study in Fanaticism. Cambridge: Harvard University Press, 1934.

Chapman, John. "Justice and Fairness," in Friedrich and Chapman, Justice Nomos VI, 1963.

Charles, Alan and Susan Alexander, "Abortions for Poor and Non-White Women: A Denial of Equal Protection?" Hastings Law Journal 23: 147-69, November 1971.

Chesney-Lind, M. "Protest Motherhood: Pregnancy Decision-Making Behavior and Attitudes Towards Abortion". Paper presented at Annual Meeting of American Sociological Association, Boston, 1979.

Chomsky, Noam. Problems of Knowledge and Freedom. New York: Pantheon Books, 1971.

Choptiany, L., "Critique of John Rawl's Principle of Justice," Ethics, 83: 146-50, January, 1973.

Cicero. De Inventione. Friedrich, (ed) Leipzig: B. G. Teubner, 1884.

Cicourel, Aaron. Method and Measurement in Sociology. New York: Free Press, 1964.

Cisler, L., "Abortion Law Repeal (sort of), Notes (From the Second Year) Radical Feminism, 1970.

Cohen, J., et al. The Rights and Wrongs of Abortion. Princeton, N.J.: Princeton University Press, 1974.

Cohen, Julius. "Perspectives on the Limits of Law," in Pennock and Chapman, The Limits of Law, 1974.

Coleman, J. S. "Inequality, Sociology, and Moral Philosophy" (Review Article), American Journal of Sociology, 80: 739-64, November, 1974.

Combs, M. and S. Welch. "Blacks, Whites and Attitudes Toward Abortion." Public Opinion Quarterly, 46, 1982.

Cooke, Robert, Andre Hellegers, Robert Hoyt, and Herbert Richardson, (eds). The Terrible Choice: The Abortion Dilemma. New York: Bantam, 1968.

Coser, Lewis and Bernard Rosenberg. Sociological Theory. New York: MacMillan and Co., 1964.

Cotta, Sergio. "Law Between Ethics and Politics: A Phenomenological Approach," in Pennock and Chapman (eds) The Limits of Law, 1974.

Craig, L. H. "Contra Contract: A Brief Against John Rawl's Theory of Justice," Canadian Journal Political Science, 8: 63-81, March, 1975.

Curran, C. E. "Abortion: Its Moral Aspects." In William E. Batchelor. Abortion: The Moral Issues. New York: Pilgrim Press, 1982.

Curran, William, "The Legal Authority of Health Departments to Regulate Abortion Practice," American Journal of Public Health, 61: 621-26, March, 1971.

Cutler, D. (ed) Updating Life and Death. Boston: Beacon Press, 1969.

Cutler, S. J., et al. "Aging and Conservation: Cohort Changes in Attitudes About Legalized Abortion." Journal of Gerontology, 35: 115-123, 1980.

Cutler, S. J., et al. "Cohort Chages in Attitudes Abouts Legalized Abortion." Paper presented at The Conference of the Gerontological Society, San Francisco, 1978.

Darwall, S. L. "Kantian Interpretation" O. A. Johnson Ethics 85: 58-66 October, 1974.
Reply. Ethics, 86: 164-70, Januray, 1976.

Davis, Kingsley, "The Population Policy: Will Current Programs Succeed?" Science, 158: 730-39, November 10, 1967.

Del Vecchio, Giorgio. Justice: An Historical and Philosophical Essay. Edinburgh: Edinburgh University Press, 1952, 1956.

D'Entreves, A. P. Natural Law. London: Hitchinson Univeristy Library. (1951) 1960.

Devereux, G. A Study of Abortion in Primitive Societies. London: T. Yoseloff, 1960.

Dike, S. Capital Punishment in the United States: A Consideration of the Evidence. Hackensack, N.J.: NCCD, 1982.

Dixon, Keith. Sociological Theory: Pretense and Possibility. London: Routledge and K. Paul, 1973.

Dostoyevsky, F. Crime and Punishment. Baltimore, MD: Penguin, 1951.

Douglas, Jack. Understanding Everyday Life Toward the Reconstruction of Sociological Knowledge. Chicago: Aldine Publishing Co., 1970.

Drinan, Robert, "Should There Be Laws Against Abortions?" U. S. Catholic, April, 1970, p. 15-19.

Drinan, Robert, "The Right of the Fetus to be Born." Dublin Review #514, Winter 1967-1968.

Duguit, L. "Collective Acts as Distinguished from Contracts." Yale Law Journal, 27, 1918.

Durkheim, Emile. On Morality and Society. Selected Writings. Robert Bellah (ed). Chicago/London: The University of Chicago Press, 1973.

Dupre, L. The Philosophical Foundations of Marxism. New York: Harcourt, Bruce and World, Inc., 1966.

Ebaugh, H. and C. A. Haney. "Shifts in Abortion Attitudes: 1972-1978." Journal of Marriage and Family, 42, 1980.

Eckhoff, Torstein. Justice: Its Determinates in Social Interaction. Rotterdam: Rotterdam University Press, 1974.

Ehrlich, Paul and Anne Ehrlich. Population/Resources/-Environment. San Francisco: W. H. Freeman, 1970.

Ekelund, R. B. and R. D. Tollison. "New Political Economy of J. S. Mill: The Means to Social Justice," Canadian Journal of Economics, 9: 213-31, May, 1076.

Evers, M. and J. McGee. "The Trend and Pattern in Attitudes Toward Abortion in the U.S.: 1965-1977." Social Indication Research, 7, 1980.

Faulkner, Robert. "Spontaneity, Justice and Coercion: On Nichomachean Ethics, Books III and V," in Pennock and Chapman (eds) Coercion. Chicago: Aldine, 1972.

Feinberg, J., "Duty and Obligation in the Non-Ideal World" (Review Article) J. Philos 70: 263-75, May 10, 1973.

Felton, Gerald and Roy Smith, "Administrative Guidelines For An Abortion Service," American Journal of Nursing, 72: 108-9, January, 1972.

Filmer, Paul, Michael Phillipson, et al. New Directions in Sociological Theory. Cambridge, Mass.: M.I.T. Press, 1972.

Filstead, William (ed). Qualitative Methodology: Firsthand Involvement with The Social World. Chicago: Markham Publishing Co., 1970.

Finnis, John. "The Rights and Wrongs of Abortion," Philosophy and Public Affairs. Cohen, Nagel and Scanlon (eds), Princeton: Princeton University Press, 1974.

Finnis, John. "Three Schemes of Regulation," The Morality of Abortion: Legal and Historical Perspectives. John T. Noonan, Jr., (ed). Cambridge: Harvard University Press, 1970.

Flathman, Richard. The Public Interest: An Essay Concerning the Normative Discourse of Politics. New York: Wiley, 1966.

Fleck, Stephen, "Some Psychiatric Aspects of Abortion," Journal of Nervous and Mental Disease. 151: 42-50, July, 1970

Fletcher, J. "Abortion and the True Believer." In E. Batcherlor. Abortion: The Moral Issues. New York: Pilgrim Press, 1982.

Flew, A. "Social Virtue and Blind Justice: On John Rawl's Theory," Encounter, 41: 73-6, November, 1973.

Flynn, James. Humanism and Ideology. Boston: Routledge and Kegan Paul, 1973.

Forssman, Hans and Inga Thuwe, "One Hundred and Twenty Children Born After Application for Therapeutic Abortion Refused." In C. Reiterman. Abortion and the Unwanted Child. New York: Springer, 1971.

Foucault, M. Discipline and Punishment. New York: Vintage, 1979.

Freud, S. Group Psychology and the Analysis of the Ego. London: Hogarth Press, 1948 (Translated by J. Strachey).

Freud, S. Totem and Taboo. New York: W. W. Norton, 1952. (Translated by J. Strachey).

Fried, Charles. "Justice and Liberty," in Friedrich and Chapmen (eds), Justice Nomos VI, New York: Atherton Press, 1963.

Friedrich, Carl and John Chapman, (ed) Justice Nomes VI. New York: Atherton Press, 1963.

Friedrich, Carl. Rational Decision. New York: Atherton Press, 1967.

Fromm, Erich. Marx's Concept of Man. New York: Frederick Ungar Publishing Company, 1966.

Fuller, L. E. "American Legal Philosophy at Mid Century" in Journal Legal Education, 6: 457-68, 1954.

Furstenburg, F. F., "Attitudes Toward Abortion Among Young Blacks," Studies in Family Planning, 3: 66-69, April, 1972.

Gardner, R. F. R. Abortion: The Personal Dilema. Grand Rapids: William B. Eerdmans Publishing Co., 1972.

Garlan, Edwin. Legal Realism and Justice. New York: Columbia University Press, 1941.

Gastil, R. D. "Beyond a Theory of Justice," Ethics, 85: 183-94, April, 1975.

Geerken, M. and W. Gove. "Deterrence: Some Theoretical Considerations." Law and Society Review, 9, 1975.

George, J. "Current Abortion Laws: Proposals and Movement for Reform," in David T. Smith, (ed). Abortion and the Law. Cleveland: Press of Western Reserve University, 1967, p. 17-18.

Gerwirth, A. "Obligation: Political, Legal and Moral." In S. Hook (Ed). Law and Philosophy. New York: New York University Press, 1964.

Giddens, Anthony. Positivism and Sociology. London: Heinemann, 1974.

Ginsberg, Morris. On Justice in Society. Baltimore: Penguin Books, 1963.

Ginsberg, Morris. "The Concept of Justice," Philosophy,

XXXVIII (1963) p. 99-116.

Glaser, Barney G. and Anselm L. Strauss. The Discovery of Grounded Theory: Strategies for Qualitative Research. Chicago: Aldine Publishing Company, 1967.

Goldberg, Arthur. Equal Justice, Evanston, Ill.: Northwestern University Press, 1971.

Goldman, A. H. "Limits of the Justification of Reverse Discrimination," Soc. Theory and Pract., 3: 289-306, Spring, 1975.

Gordon, S., "John Rawl's Difference Principle, Utilitarianism and The Optimum Degree of Inequality," Journal of Philosophy, 70: 275-80, May 10, 1973.

Gouldner, A., "Norm of Reciprocity," American Sociological Review, 25: 161-178, 1960.

Granfield, David. The Abortion Decision. New York: Doubleday, 1969.

Green, T. H. Principles of Political Obligation, 1901.

Greer, G. and K. Keating. "What's Happening to the American Family?" Better Homes and Gardens, 56, 1978.

Gregory, Dick, "My Answer to Genocide," Ebony, October 1971, pp. 66-72.

Grisez, Germain. Abortion: The Myths, The Realities and the Arguments. New York: Corpus Books, 1970.

Grotius, Hugo. De June Belli al Pacis Libri Tres. Paris, 1625. Translated by F. W. Kelsey and others From the 1946 edition, Oxford, 1925.

Group for the Advancement of Psychiatry. The Right to Abortion. New York: Charles Scribner's Sons, 1970.

Gurvitch, Georges. The Social Frameworks of Knowledge. Translated by Margaret Thompson. New York: Harper and Row, 1971.

Gustafson, James. "A Protestant Ethical Approach." In E. Batchelor, Abortion: The Moral Issue. New York: Pilgrim Press, 1982.

Guttmacher, Alan, (ed). The Case for Legalized Abortion Now. Berkeley: Diablo Press, 1967.

Hage, Jerald. Techniques and Problems of Theory Construction in Sociology.

Hall, Robert (ed). Abortion in a Changing World. New York: Columbia University Press, 1970.

Hall, Robert. "Parenthood: Rights and Privilege?" Science, 169: 419-427, December 13, 1968.

Hall, Robert. "Therapeutic Abortion, Sterilization and Contraception," American Journal of Obstetrics and Gynecology, 91, February 15, 1965.

Hammurabi, King of Babylonia. The Letters and Inscriptions of Hammurabi. (translated by L. W. King. New York: A & S Press, 1976.

Hamilton, Peter. Knowledge and Social Structure. London: and Boston: Routledge and K. Paul, 1974.

Hansen, S. et al. "Women's Political Participation and Policy Professions." Social Science Quarterly, 56, 1976.

Hardin, Garrett. "Abortion - Or Compulsory Pregnancy?" Journal of Marriage and Family, 30: 249, May, 1968.

Hardin, Garrett. "Abortion and Human Dignity," in The Case for Legalized Abortion Now, by A. Guttmacher (Ed) Berkeley: Diablo Press, 1967.

Hardin, Garrett. Stalking the Wild Taboo. Los Altos: William Kaufman, Inc., 1973.

Harris, Richard. Justice: The Crisis of Law, Order and Freedom in America. New York: E. P. Dutton, 1970.

Harrison, B. E. "Theology of Pre-Choice: A Feminist Perspective" in E. Batchelor, Abortion: The Moral Issues. New York: Pilgrim Press, 1982.

Hart, Harold, (ed). Censorship For or Against. New York: Hart, 1971.

Hartmann, Nicolai. Ethics. London: Allen and Unwin Co., 1932.

Hecker, Eugene. A Short History of Woman's Rights. Westport: Greenwood Press, revised ed, 1971.

Hegel, G. Philosophy of Right. Trans. by T. Knox. Oxford: Clarendon Press, 1945.

Held, Virginia. The Public Interest and The Indivitual Interest. New York: Basic Book. 1970.

Hempel, Carl G. Fundamental of Concept Formation in Empirical Science. Chicago, Ill.: The University of Chicago Press, 1952.

Henry, Michel. The Essence of Manifestation. Translated from French by Girard Etzkorn. The Hague: Nijhoff, 1973.

Henry, Nannere, "Political Obligation and Collective Goods," in Pennock and Chapman (eds), Politica and Legal Obligation, 1970.

Hilgers, Thomas and Dennis Horan. Abortion and Social Justice. New York: Sheed and Ward, 1972.

Hobbes, T. The Levianthan. Oxford: Clarendon Press, 1947.

Hobhouse, L. The Elements of Social Justice. London: Allen and Unwin, 1949.

Hoffman, Robert. Revolutionary Justice. Chicago: University of Ill. Press, 1972.

Holmes, O. W. cited in The Myths, The Realities and The Arguments, by Germain Grisez, New York: Corpus Books, 1970.

Holmes, O. W. "Law in Science and Science in Law." Harvard Law Review, 12, 1927.

Holmes, O. W. "The Path of the Law." Harvard Law Review, 10, 1897.

Homans, George. Social Behavior: Its Elementary Forms. New York: Harcourt, Brace and World, Inc., 1961, 1974.

Honderick, Ted. Punishment: The Supposed Justification. Baltimore: Penguin Books, 1971.

Hook, S. Law and Philosophy. New York: New York University Press, 1964.

Horowitz, Irving, "Social Science Objectivity and Value Neutrality: Historical Problems and Projections," Diogenes, 39:17-44, Fall, 1962.

Hourani, George. "Thrasymachus' Definition of Justice in Plato's Republic," Phronesis, VII, 1962, p. 111.

Hughes, Graham (ed). Law, Reason and Justice. New York: New York University Press, 1969.

Hume, D. An Enquiry Concerning The Principles of Morals. Selby-Biggs, (ed) Oxford: Clarendon Press, 1894.

Hume, D. A Treatise of Human Nature. Oxford: Clarendon Press, 1955.

Hume, D. Human Nature. Garden City, N.J.: Doubleday Dolphin, 1961.

Hunt, Earl B. Concept Learning: An Information Processing Problem. New York: Wiley, 1962.

Husserl, Edmund. The Idea of Phenomenology. Translated by William P. Alston and George Nekhnikian. The Hague: Nijhoff, 1964.

Husserl, Edmund. Logical Investigations. Translated by J. N. Findlay from The 2nd German Edition. London: Routledge and Kegan Paul. New York: Humanities Press, 1970.

Huxley, Julian. Knowledge, Morality and Destiny. New York: Mentor, 1960.

Ihering, R. Law as a means to an End, 1913.

International Social Science Journal. Decisions and Decision-Makers in The Modern State. Zurich: Unesco, 1967.

Jacob, P. E. and J. J. Flink, and Schuchman, "Values and Their Function in Decision-Making" in American Behavioral Scientist, 5: 1962.

Jaffee, F. S., et al. Abortion Politics: Private Morality and Public Policy. New York: McGraw, Hill, 1981.

Jones, W. T. Morality and Freedom in the Philosophy of Immanuel Kant. London: Oxford University Press, 1940.

Jones, E. and C. Westoff. "How Attitudes Toward Abortion are Changing." Journal of Population. 1, 1978.

Kant, Immanual. "General Introduction to the Metaphysic of Morals" in Great Books of the Western World. Chicago:

175

Encyclopedia Britannica, Inc. 1952, vol. 42.

Kant, Immanual. Foundations of the Metaphysics of Morals. Trans by L. Beck, III.: Bobbs Merrill, Co., 1959.

Kant, Immanual. Philosophy of Law, 1884.

Kaplan, Abraham. The Conduct of Inquiry. San Francisco: Chanlder, 1964.

Katzner, Isaac, An Analysis of the Concept of Justice, Dissertation. Ann Arbor: University of Michigan, 1968.

Katzner, Isaac, "Presumption of Reasons and Presumptions of Justice," J. Phil., 70: 89-100, February 22, 1973.

Kelly, Edmond. Government or Human Evolution: Justice. London: Longmans, Green and Co., 1900.

Kelly, Edmond. "Government or Human Evolution-Justice. In Del Vecchio, Justice. Edinburgh: Edenburgh University Press, 1952.

Kelsen, Hans. General Theory of Law and State. New York: Russell and Russell, 1961.

Kelsen, Hans. What Is Justice? Berkeley: University of California Press, 1957.

Kendler, Tracy St. "Concept Formation," Annual Review of Psychology. 12, 1961, p. 447-472.

Kent, Allen. Law and Philosophy. New York: Meredith Corp., 1970, p. 464.

Kline, George, "Socialist Legality and Communist Ethics," Natural Law Forum, VIII (1963), p. 21-34.

Kluckhohn, F.; F. Strodtbeck. Variations in Value Orientation. Evanston, Ill.: Row, Peterson, 1971.

Kluge, Eike-Henner. The Practice of Death. New Haven: Yale University Press, 1975.

Kohler, J. Philosophy of Law, 1914 (Translated by Albrecht).

Krannich, R. S. "Abortion in the U.S.: Past, Present and Future Trends." Family Relations, 29, 1980.

Kuhn, T. The Structure of Scientific Revolution. Chicago: University of Chicago Press, 1970.

Lacy, J. R., "Sidgwick's Ethics Maxims," Philosophy XXXIX (1959), p. 217-228.

Ladd, John. "Law and Morality," in S. Hook (Ed) Law and Philosophy. New York: New York University Press, 1964.

Lader, Lawrence. Abortion. Boston: Beacon Press, 1967.

Lader, Lawrence. "The New Abortion Laws: A Discussion of the Ethical and Medical Considerations that Underlie," Parent's Magazine, April, 1968.

Lader, Lawrence. Abortion II: Making the Revolution. Boston: Beacon Press, 1973.

Laird, J. Hume's Philosophy of Human Nature. London: Methuen, 1932.

Lakoff, Stanford. Equality in Political Philosophy. Boston: Beacon Press, 1964.

Lee, Harold. Precepts, Concepts and Theoretical Knowledge. Memphis: Memphis State University Press, 1973.

Leibniz, G., "On the Notions of Right and Justice," Philosophical Papers and Letters. Loemker, (ed)., Chicago: University of Chicago Press, 1956.

Lenin, V. I. Materialism and Empiro - Criticism in Collected Works. New York: International Publishers, 1927-1942.

Lerner, M. J. (ed) "Justice Motive in Social Behavior," (Symposium). Journal of Social Issues, 31 no. 3: 1-20, 1975.

Lieberman, Jethro. The Tyranny of the Experts. New York: Walker, 1970.

Life, April 30, 1965.

Lincoln, Richard, "S. 2108: Capital Hill Debates the Future of Population and Family Planning," Family Planning Perspectives, 2: 6-12, January, 1970.

Lindsay. Karl Marx Capital: An Introductory Essay. Oxford: Clarendon Press, 1942.

Linton, R. The Study of Man. New York: Appleton, Century, 1940.

Lipset, S. M. Political Man. New York: Doubleday and Co., 1959, p. 24.

Lobenthal, Jr., Joseph. Power and Put-On. New York: Outerbridge and Dienstfrey, 1970.

Locke, J. Two Treatises on Civil Government. New York: E. P. Dutton, 1943.

Locke, J. Essays on the Law of Nature. Von Leyden (ed), Oxford: Clarendon Press, 1958.

Lodge, R. C. Plato's Theory of Ethics. London: Routledge and Kegan Paul. 1926.

Louisell, David and J. Noonan, "Constitutional Balance," In J. T. Noonan The Morality of Abortion: Legal Historical Perceptions, Cambridge: Harvard University Press, 1970.

Luizpen, William. Phenomenology of Natural Law. Pittsburgh, Pa.: Duquesne University, 1967.

Lynd, Robert. Knowledge for What? New York: Grove Press Edition, 1964.

Machiavelli, Niccolo. The Prince. Trans. by W. K. Marriott. New York: Dulton Everyman's Library, (1908), 1968.

Mack, E., "Distribution Versus Justice," Ethics, 86: 145-53, January, 1976.

Mankekar, Kamla. Abortion the Social Dilemma. London: Vikas Publishing House, 1973.

Mannes, Mayra, "A Woman Views Abortion," in A. Guttmacher The Case for Legalized Abortion Now, Berkeley: Diablo Press, 1967.

Mannheim, Karl. Systematic Sociology. New York: Grove Press, 1957.

Maritain, J. Man and The State. Chicago: University of Chicago Press, 1951.

Maritain, J. The Rights of Man and Natural Lay. New York: Scribner's Sons, 1943.

Marcuse, Soviet Marxism: A Critical Analysis. New York: Columbia University Press, 1958.

Markovic, Mihailo, "Marxist Humanism and Ethics," Inquiry, VI (1963) p. 18-34.

Mason, Sheila Mary. Monteequeren's Idea of Justice. Hague, Netherlands: Martenus Nijhoff, 1975.

Marx, K. and F. Engels. The German Ideology. New York: International Publishers, 1947.

Marx, Karl. Capital. Moscow: Foreign Language Publishing House, 1959.

Marx, Karl. Economic and Philosophical Manuscripts. Trans. by T. B. Bottomore. London: Watt, 1962.

Marx, K. and F. Engels. Selected Works, Volume 1 and 2. London, 1951.

Marx, Karl. Selected Writings in Sociology and Social Philosophy. Translated by T. B. Bottomore. New York: McGraw Hill Book Co., 1956.

McBridge, W. L., "Concept of Justice in Marx, Engels, and others," Ethics, 85: 204-18, April 1975.

McCloskey, H. J., "Equalitarianism, Equality and Justice," Australasian Journal of Philosophy. XLIV (1966), p. 50-69.

McCormick, Patricia. Attitudes Toward Abortion. Lexington, Mass.: Lexington Books, 1975.

McEwin, William. The Problem of Social-Scientific Knowledge. London: Bedminster, 1963.

McKeon, Richard, "Justice and Equality," in Friedrich and Chapman (eds) Justics Nomos VI.

Mead, M. "Right to Life". In E. Batchelor Abortion: The Moral Issues. New York: Pilgrim, 1982.

Means, C. "The Phoenix of Abortion Freedom: Is a Penumbral or Ninth-Amendment Right About to Arise from the Nineteenth-Century Legislative Ashes of Fourteenth Century Common-Law Liberty?" New York Law Forum, 17, 1971, pp. 392-96.

Means, Cyril, "The Law of New York Concerning Abortion and The Status of The Fetus, 1664-1968: A Case of Cessation of Constitutionality," New York Law Forum, 14, 1968..

Mecklenburg, F. "The Indications for Induced Abortion" in Abortion and Social Justice. Hilgers and Horan (eds). New York: Sheed and Ward, 1972.

Merino, Daniel. Natural Justice and Private Property. St. Louis: Herder, 1923.

Mill, John Stuart. Utilitarianism. New York: Appleton, Century Crofts, 1957.

Mill, John Stuart. "On liberty" in Essays on Politics and Society. Edited by J. Robson. Toronto: University of Toronto Press, 1977.

Miller, D., "Ideological Background to Conceptions of Social Justice," Pol. Stud., 22: 387-99, December, 1974.

Mitford, J. Kind and Usual Punishment. New York: Vintage, 1973.

Mohanty, J. N. Phenomenology and Ontology. The Hague: Nijhoff, 1970.

Moquet, Jacques J. The Sociology of Knowledge, Its Structure and Its Relation To The Philosophy of Knowledge: A Critical Analysis of The Systems of Karl Mannheim and Pitirim Sorokin. Boston: Beacon (1949) 1951.

Morgenthau, H. J., "Justice and Power," Soc. Res., 41: 163-75, Spring, 1974.

Morris, Clarence, "Law, Justice and The Public's Aspiration." In Friedrich and Chapman (eds), Justice - Nomos VI, New York: Atherton Press, 1963.

Mosca, G. The Ruling Class. Trans. by H. D. Kahn. New York: McGraw-Hill Books, Co., Inc. 1939.

Naumann, C. E. and C. McDiarmid. "Changes in the Feminist Perspective: From 1970-1980." Paper presented at Annual Convention of the Association for Women in Psychology, Boston, 1981.

Neuberger, M. "Abortion: a Political View" in Abortion and the Unwanted Child by Carl Reiterman (ed). New York: Springer Publishing Co., Inc., 1971.

Newman, Jeremiah. Conscience versus Law. Chicago: Franciscan Harold Press, 1971.

Newman, G. The Punishment Response. New York: J. B.

Lippincott, 1978.

Niebuhr, R. Moral Man and Immoral Society: A Study in Ethics and Politics. New York: Scribner, 1982.

Noonan, John. The Morality of Abortion: Legal and Historical Perspectives. Cambridge, MA: Harvard University Press, 1970.

Olafson, Frederick. Justice and Social Policy. Englewoods Cliffs, N.Y.: Prentice Hall, 1961.

Palmer, J. "Economic Analysis of the Deterrent Effects of Punishment: A Review." Journal of Research on Crime and Delinquency. 14, 1977.

Pareto, V. The Mind and Society. Livingston, (ed), New York: Harcourt, Brace and Co., 1935.

Parsons, Talcott. The Social System. New York: Free Press, 1951.

Parsons, Talcott. Social Structure and Personality. New York: Free Press, 1964.

Patterson, Janet, & R. C. Patterson. Abortion The Trojan Horse. New York: Thomas Nelson, Inc. 1974.

Paul, Julius. "The Return of Punitive Sterilization Proposals: Current Attacks on Illegitimacy and the AFDC Program, "Law and Society Review", August, 1968.

Pennock, J. Roland and Chapman, J., (eds). Coercion. Chicago/New York: Aldine/Atherton, Inc., 1972.

Pennock, J. and Chapmann, J., Equality. New York, New York: Atherton, 1967.

Pennock, J. Political and Legal Obligation. New York: Atherton Press, 1970.

Pennock, J. The Limits of Law. New York: Lieber Atherton, 1974.

Pepper, S. The Sources of Values. Berkeley: University of California Press, 1958.

Perelman, C. The Idea of Justice and the Problem of Argument. New York: The Humanities Press, 1963.

Perelman, C. Justice. New York: Random House, 1967.

Piaget, Jean. The Moral Judgment of the Child. Trans. by
Marjorie Gabain. New York: Collier Books, 1962.

Piaget, Jean. The Moral Judgment of the Child. London:
Routledge and Kegan Paul, 1932.

Plamenatz, F. P. Consent, Freedom and Political Obligation.
London: Oxford, 1968.

Plant, B. "A Survey of the U.S. Abortion Literature,
1890-1970" MA Thesis, University of Windsor, Ontario,
1971; Cited in Samuist Rodman The Abortion
Controversy. New York: Columbia University Press,
1974.

Plato. The Republic. Trans. by F. Cornford. Oxford:
Clarendon Press, 1892.

Popper, K. The Open Society and Its Enemies. VIII.
(Formerly The High Tide of Prophecy. Hegel, Marx and
the Aftermath. New York: Harper Torch Books, 1963.

Potter, Ralph, "The Abortion Debate," in Donald Cutler,
Updating Life and Death: Essays in Ethics and
Medicine. Boston: Beacon 1969.

Pound, R. Introduction to the Philosophy of Law. New
Haven, CT: Yale, 1922.

Pound, R. Social Control Through Law. Anchor Books,
1968.

Prager, E. "Playing God." Penthouse, 13, 1981.

Proudhon, Pierre-Joseph. What is Property? Princeton, 1976
(Translated by B. Tucker).

Pritchard, M. S. "Human Dignity and Justice," Ethics, 82:
299-313.

Psatha, George. Phenomenological Sociology: Issues and
Applications. New York: Wiley, 1973.

Prosch, H. "The Problem of Ultimate Justification," in
International Journal of Ethics, 71: 155-74, 1961.

Radbrush, G. The Legal Philosophies of Lask, Radbrush and
Dakin. Cambridge, 1950.

Ramsey, Paul, "Reference Points in Deciding about Abortion,"
The Morality of Abortion, op. cit., pp. 60-100.

Rawls, John. "Legal Obligation and the Duty of Fair Play." in S. Hook (Ed). Law and Philosophy. New York: New York University Press, 1964.

Rawls, John. A Theory of Justice. Cambridge, Harvard University Press, 1971.

Rawls, John. "Justics as Fairness," The Philosophical Review, 67: 164-194, 1958.

Rawls, John. "The Sense of Justice," The Philosophical Review, 72: 281-305, 1963.

Regan, D. "Rewriting Roe v. Wade." In C. E. Schneider and M. A. Vinovskis. The Law and Politics of Abortion. Lexington, Lexington Books, 1980.

Reeves, Nancy. Womankind. Chicago/New York: Aldine/-Atherton, 1971.

Riesman, D. The Lonely Crowd. Garden City, N.J.: oubleday, 1952.

Reiterman, C. Abortion and the Unwanted Child. New York: Springer, 1971.

Rescher, Nicholas. Distributive Justice. New York: Bobbs Merrill, 1966.

Robinson, J., et al. Measure of Political Attitudes. Ann Arbor, MI: Institute for Social Research, 1969.

Roe, V. Wade, 410 U.S. 113 (1973).

Rose, A. "A Systematic Summary of Symbolic Interaction Theory", in Human Behavior and Social Processes by A. M. Rose (ed), 1962.

Rosenfeld, A. The Second Genesis: The Coming Control of Life. Englewood Cliffs, N.J.: Prentice Hall, 1969.

Ross, Alf. On Law and Justice. Berkeley: University of California Press, 1959.

Ross, E. A. Social Control. New York: MacMillan, 1916.

Rosseau, Jean-Jacques. Contract social, 1762.

Rossi, Alice, "Abortion Laws and their Victims," Transaction. September-October, 1966.

Rougier, L., "Philosophical Origins of the Ideal of Natural Equality," Modern Age., 18: 29-38, Winter, 1974.

Rubin, E. Abortion, Politics, and the Courts: Roe v. Wade and Its Aftermath. Westport, CT: Greenwood Press, 1982.

Runciman, W. G. Relative Deprivation and Social Justice. London: Routledge and Kegan Paul, 1966.

Russell, David. Children's Thinking. Boston: Ginn, 1956.

Sarvis, Betty and Hyman Rodman. The Abortion Controversy. New York: Columbia University Press, 1974.

Schneider, C. E. and M. A. Vinovskis. The Law and Politics of Abortion. Lexington, Lexington Books, 1980.

Schopenhauer, A. On the Basis of Morality. Trans. by E. Paine. Indianapolis: Liberal Arts Press, 1965.

Schur, Edwin. Law and Society: A Sociological View. New York: Random House, 1968.

Schur, Edwin. "Abortion and the Social System in E. Schur (Ed). The Family and the Sexual Revolution. Bloomington, IN.: Indiana University Press, 1964.

Schur, Edwin. Crimes Without Victims: Deviant Behavior and Public Policy. Englewood Cliffs: Prentice Hall, 1965.

Schulder, Diane and Florence Kennedy. Abortion Rap. New York: McGraw Hill, 1971.

Schutz, Alfred. "Concepts and Theory Formation in the Social Sciences," The Journal of Philosophy, 51: 257-73, 1954.

Schutz, Alfred. The Phenomenology of the Social World. Trans. by Lehnert Walsh. Evanston, Ill.: Northwestern University, 1967.

Schwartz, Murry, "The Separation of Legal and Moral Decisions," in Friedrich (ed), National Decision, 1967.

Schwartz, A. "Moral Neutrality and Primary Good" Ethics, 83: 294-307, July 1973.

Schwartz, Richard and Jerome H. Skolnick (eds), Society and The Legal Order/Cases and Materials in the Sociology of Law. New York/London: Basic Books, 1970.

Segerstedt, Torgny. The Nature of Social Reality, An Essay in the Epistemology of Empirical Sociology. London: Bedminster, 1966.

Seligman, David. Justice and The Role of Retribution in Punishment. Thesis Columbia Unvieristy Microfilm of Typescript. Ann Arbor: Michigan University Press Microfilms, 1966.

Selsam, Howard. Socialism and Ethics. New York: International Publishers, 1943.

Seymour, Whitney, Jr. Why Justice Fails. New York: William Marrow and Company, 1973.

Shaw, Russell. Abortion on Trial. Ohio: Pflaum Press, 1968.

Shainess, Natalie, "Abortion Is No Man's Business," Psychology Today, 3: 18, May, 1970.

Shainess, Natalie, "Abortion: Inalienable Right," New York State Journal of Medicine, 1: 1772-1775, July, 1972.

Sidgwick, H. Method of Ethics. London: MacMillan and Co., 1962.

Sidgwick, H. Elements of Politics. London: MacMillan, 1897.

Singer, Marcus, "Hart's Concept of Law," Journal of Philosophy. 60: 197-220, 1963.

Smith, A. The Wealth of Nations. New York: Modern Library, 1937.

Smith, Bruce and L. K. and D. Hague (eds). The Dilemma of Accountability in Modern Government. New York: MacMillan, 1971.

Smith, R. J. "Human Life Bell Arouses More Opposition." Science, 212, 1981.

Solomon, M. "Redemptive Rhetoric: The Continuity Motel in the Rhetoric of Right to Life." Central States Speech Journal, 31, 1980.

Sorokin, P. Social and Cultural Dynamics. New York: American Book Co., 1937-1941.

Sorrentino, J. the Moral Revolution. Los Angeles: Nash Publishing Co., 1972.

Spencer, Herbert. Synthetic Philosophy, Justice: Part IV of Ethics. New York: Appleton, 1892.

Stace, W. T. The Concept of Morals. New York: MacMillan, 1937.

Stammler, R. The Theory of Justice, Trans. by Isaac Musik. New York: MacMillan Co., 1925.

Stevenson, C. Ethics and Language. New Haven: Yale University Press, 1944.

Stapleton, Lawrence. Justice and World Society. Chapel Hill: The University of North Carolina Press, 1944.

St. John-Stevas, Norman. The Right to Life. New York: Holt, Rinehart and Winston, 1964.

Stephen, L. The English Utilitarians. London: Duckworth, 1900

Strauss, L. Natural Right and History. Chicago: Univeristy of Chicago Press, 1953.

Stevenson, Charles. Ethics and Language. New Haven: Yale University Press, 1944.

Stone, J. Human Law and Human Justice. Stanford: Stanford University Press, 1965.

Stone, J. Social Dimensions of Law and Justice. Stanford: Stanford University Press, 1966.

Stoll, A. "Mill's Fallacy," Dialogue, III (1965), p. 835-404.

Sumner, L. W. "Toward a Credible View of Abortion." Canadian Journal of Philosophy, 14, 1974.

Sumner, L. W. Abortion and Moral Theory. Princeton, N.J.: Princeton University Press, 1981.

Sutherland, E. H. and D. R. Cressey. Criminology. New York: J. B. Lippincott, 1978.

Symposium, "A Theory of Justice: John Rawl's", J. Philos., 69: 535-57, October 5, 1972.

Symposium, "Plato on the Language of Justice," J. Philos. 69: 557-59, October 5, 1972.

Szasz, Thomas, "The Ethics of Abortion," Humanist,
    September-October 1966, p. 148.

Taussig, Frederick. Abortion Spontaneous and Induced:
    Medical and Social Aspects. St. Louis: Mosby, 1936.

Tedrow, L. and E. R. Mahoney. "Trends in Attitudes Toward
    Abortion: 1972-1976." Public Opinion Quarterly, 43,
    1979.

Tillich, Paul. Love, Power, Justice. Oxford: Oxford
    University Press 1954.

Tooley, Michael, "Abortion and Infanticide," in Rights and
    Wrongs of Abortion, op. cit., pp. 52-84.

Treadwell, Mary, "Is Abortion Black Genocide?" Family
    Planning Perspective, 4: 4-5, January 1972.

Thompston, J. R., "A Defense of Abortion," Philosophy and
    Public Affairs, 1: 47-66, Fall, 1971.

Thornton, W. E., J. James & W. Doerner. Delinquency and
    Justice. New York: Random House, 1982.

Tourtoulon, P. Philosophy in the Development of Law.
    Modern Legal Philosophy Seminar, 1922.

Tourtoulon, P. (See Perelman, 1963).

Tribe, David. Nucleoethics: Ethics in Modern Society.
    London: MacGivven and Kee 1972.

Tribe, David. Questions of Censorship. London: Ulen and
    Unwin, 1973.

Tucker, Robert. "Marx and Distributive Justice," in Friedrich
    and Chapman (eds), Justice-Nomos VI, 1963.

Tussman, Joseph. Obligation and the Body Politic. New
    York: Oxford University Press, 1960.

Urmson, J. O., "The Interpretation of the Moral Philosophy of
    J. S. Mill," Philosophical Quarterly, III (1953), p.
    33-39.

Van den Haag, Ernest. Punishing Criminals: Concerning a
    Very Old and Painful Question. New York: Basic
    Books, 1975.

Vinovskis, M. A. "The Politics of Abortion in the House of

Representatives in 1976" in C. E. Schneider and M. A. Vinovskis. The Law of Politics and Abortion. Lexington, 1980.

Von Hirsch, Andres. Doing Justice: The Choice of Punishment. New York: Hill and Wang, 1976.

Warrender, H. The Political Philosophy of Hobbes, His Theory of Obligation. Oxford: The Clarendon Press, 1957.

Weaver, R. The Ethics of Rhetoric. Chicago, IL: Regnory, 1953.

Weber, Max. On the Methodology of the Social Sciences. Edward A. Shils (ed), trans. Henry Finch. Glencoe, Ill.: Free Press, 1949.

Weddington, S. R. "The Woman's Right to Privacy." In E. Batchelor. Abortion: The Moral Issues. New York: Pilgrim, 1982

Wertheimer, Roger, "Understanding the Abortion Argument," Philosophy and Public Affairs, 1: 67-95, Fall 1971. (Also cited in Cohen, Nagel and Scanlon. Rights and Wrongs of Abortion. Princeton: Princeton University Press, 1974, p. 45).

Whyte, W. Street Corner Society. Chicago: University of Chicago Press, 1965.

Widmer, Eleanor. Freedom and Culture: Literary Censorship in the 70's. Belmont, CA: Wadsworth Publishing Co., 1970.

Williams, Granville. The Sanctity of Life and the Criminal Law. New York: Knof, 1957.

Williams, George, "The Sacred Condominium," The Morality of Abortion, op. cit., pp. 146-171.

Williams, J. "Abortion Condemned by Doctor as Black Genocide." Jet, 61, 1981.

Willougby, W. Social Justice: A Critical Essay. New York: MacMillan, 1900.

Wilson, Thomas. "Conceptions of Interaction and Forms of Sociological Explanation." American Sociological Review. 35: 697-710, 1970.

Wolff, Kurt. "The Sociology of Knowledge and Sociological

Theory," in Llewellyn Gross (ed.), Symposium on Sociological Theory. New York: Row Peterson, 1959.

Ziff, Paul. Semantic Analysis. Ithaca: Cornell University Press, 1960.

Zinn, Howard. Justice in Everyday Life. New York: Morrow, 1974.

Znaniecki, Florian. The Method of Sociolog. New York: Octagon Books, 1968.

Znaniecki, Florian. The Social Role of the Man of Knowledge, 1940.